SPORTS LEGENDS

For Debs, Erin and Sam – more legends
R.B.

First published in Great Britain 2021 by Walker Books Ltd
87 Vauxhall Walk, London SE11 5HJ

2 4 6 8 10 9 7 5 3 1

Text © 2021 Rick Broadbent
Cover and illustrations © 2021 James Davies

The right of Rick Broadbent and James Davies to be identified as
author and illustrator respectively of this work has been asserted by
them in accordance with the Copyright, Designs and Patents Act 1988

This book has been typeset in Bembo

Printed and bound by CPI Group (UK) Ltd, Croydon CR0 4YY

British Library Cataloguing in Publication Data:
a catalogue record for this book is
available from the British Library

ISBN 978-1-4063-9712-3

www.walker.co.uk

MIX
Paper from
responsible sources
FSC® C020471

SPORTS LEGENDS

→ **50** ←

inspiring people

to help you
reach the
top of
your
game

RICK BROADBENT

Illustrated by JAMES DAVIES

CONTENTS

WHY DOES SPORT MATTER?

I love sport because it can get you in your heart and in the pit of your stomach. It can make you feel on top of the world or at the bottom of the pile. People think it is about being physically brilliant, but that's just one part of it. The best thing about sport is how it makes you

FEEL.

In 2008, I sat in the Olympic stadium in Beijing, China and watched Usain Bolt set a new world record for the 100 metres. Think about that. At that moment in time, he wasn't just the fastest man on the planet, he was better than around 100 billion people who had lived on earth before him. Almost everybody runs at some point in their life, but nobody in any of the world's 195 countries had ever run faster. All around me in the stadium people were gasping. I actually saw people crying with joy at seeing something so spectacular.

I'm a sports journalist and it is my job to write about big events like the Olympics for a newspaper. That means as well as watching sport, I also speak to sportspeople and ask them questions. When I interviewed one of the other runners in that 100 metres final afterwards, he told me that as he waited on the starting line, it was so quiet he could hear his rivals breathing and his own heart thudding in his chest. Then the race exploded into life.

Stories like that are why I love sport. No event is ever the same. There is always noise and quiet, highs and lows, first and last, but the unpredictable nature of sport brings people together. Winning and losing is a language everyone understands.

It makes sport more gripping than any show on TV.

The drama and passion go far beyond the ten seconds it takes to run 100 metres. I'm fascinated by finding out how these people became stars. What is the story behind their success? The interesting bit is not just *what* they did on the day, but *how* they got there in the first place.

In that 100 metres race, Usain Bolt set the world record, *despite* the fact that the lace on one of his golden shoes was undone and *despite* the fact he deliberately slowed down at the end of the race to look across at his rivals and beat his chest in a gesture of triumph.

But he wasn't always the fastest runner in the world. In fact, he didn't even want to be a runner because he preferred playing cricket and football! He is very tall for a sprinter and the way his spine curves means his right leg is shorter than his left. Normally that's not great for Olympic sprinting, because you have to be perfectly balanced. So *why* did this unlikely star from Jamaica decide he wanted to compete against athletes who were training in expensive academies in America and Europe? And then *how* did he beat them?

Trying to answer questions like these is why I think I have the best job in the world. I have written about the Olympic Games, the football and rugby World Cups, Formula 1 races, world title boxing clashes and big tennis tournaments. I've visited more than 40 countries and I've been lucky enough to meet hundreds of sportspeople – some mega-famous and some almost unknown – and listen to their stories about how and why they've got to where they are today.

I have watched legends like Lionel Messi do incredible things on a football pitch that make your mind boggle and your jaw drop. But what really fascinates me is how little Leo from Rosario in Argentina got to the top at all.

As a boy, Messi didn't grow at the same rate as other kids. Doctors diagnosed him with a hormone deficiency syndrome that meant he would need regular injections to make him grow at a normal rate. But it cost $1,000 (US) for a 45-day programme and his family didn't have that sort of money. Then, when he was ten, Messi's beloved grandmother died and he was devastated. Yet, only five years later, he was in the Barcelona first team. I wondered how a small, shy boy, with an underlying health condition and grieving for his grandmother had become the greatest footballer in the world.

What Bolt and Messi had in common was two things: they had determination and they had a dream.

Behind the fame and glory, it is the mental strength that sports legends have that amazes me – and I think it can help us in our everyday lives too. You don't have to win the Ballon d'Or or stand on top of the Olympic podium to feel like a champion. You can do it by scoring a goal in your next match or getting a new personal best on the track or in the pool.

I wanted to write a book that would give you an insight into the minds of some of the greatest sportspeople on the planet. I hope that their incredible stories will show you that you too can overcome almost anything. I also want you to see that you can reach the top of your game by using the same mind tricks.

So, why did I choose these legends out of all the ones I have watched and interviewed over the years? Well, I decided to keep the stories to people I have met (or at least family members and those close to them) so I could give you an insight into what they are really like. Some are global superstars and others you might not have heard of. What unites these stories are their important messages. They are stories that make us remember there is no such thing as failure if we learn from mistakes. They are stories that can help us face our fears, be more confident, change our negative thinking and dare to be ourselves. If we listen to these legends then we will never give up.

Imagine the mental strength you need to be Paul Vice, a soldier who almost died after a bomb went off. He was badly injured in the blast and eventually had to have his leg amputated. He thought his life as he knew it was over, but then he discovered motor racing. He found a new purpose and began competing in a specially modified car.

I hope these stories will help you discover your dream and fight for it with the same determination. These legends have overcome their fears and failures and found their confidence, often when the odds have been against them.

Think of these people as your brain trainers who will help you be the best that you can be. They will show you what to do when things are hard. You don't have to be a superstar to get through whatever life throws at you. But you can use the mindset of a champion to reach the top of your game.

CHAPTER 1:
FACING FEAR

Let's start with a simple question: what are you afraid of?

Fear can stop us from reaching our full potential in life. It might help to know we are all afraid of something – even those people that we think are the strongest and bravest.

It's not nice. Fear can make you feel sick. It can make you want to pull the covers back over your head and not bother with going to school. It can make you want to run away. It can make you refuse to try something new.

There are thousands of things that make people afraid. Did you know that Serena Williams, the brilliant tennis player, is afraid of the dark? Or that Dennis Bergkamp, the great Arsenal and Dutch footballer, was scared of flying? If his team was playing an away match in Europe he would spend days travelling there by train and car. Rebecca Adlington won an Olympic swimming title, but she would never go in the sea because she was frightened of what was underneath her. Others were scared of failure or being embarrassed. The list goes on.

Fear is an emotion caused by the threat of danger, harm or pain. It can affect pretty much any part of your life. It's useful for keeping you out of trouble – you wouldn't put your hand in a fire for fear of getting burnt – but it can be horrible too. Fear can hold you back from trying new things or pushing yourself to be the best you can be.

I know what it's like. I used to be really quiet at school and I hated being asked a question by the teacher. My throat would become dry and I'd start sweating as I tried to answer. Now, all these years on, I have spoken on the radio and TV, and in front of hundreds of people. I learnt to get over my fear and now I look back and wonder what I was afraid of. But at the time it was an awful feeling.

Now you might think what has all this fear stuff got to do with the legends in this book? Well, the fact is that years of interviewing the top sports stars has made me realize that even those people we think are superheroes are often afraid of things.

The best sports stars in the world suffer from nerves and anxiety, just like you or me. I've met footballers who were frightened they would let their teammates down or play badly and get dropped by the manager and sold to another team. Lots of sportspeople get scared they will mess up and embarrass themselves in front of the crowds. Some get so anxious before a big game or race, they throw up.

So how do legends face their fears? What drives them to take chances, to compete in front of thousands of people and risk failure day in and day out?

In this chapter I will introduce you to the Olympic swimmer who used to be scared of water. Then he buried his fear of failure by using the story of a famous Spanish general who played an incredible mind trick on his soldiers. He learnt to

BURN THE BOATS!

There is the teenage girl who came back from one of the most astonishing motorsport crashes ever seen to race again. She now fears nothing. When you become resilient,

YOU CAN HANDLE IT.

I'm going to tell you about meeting one of the world's most famous rugby players who had won everything there was to win in his sport, including the World Cup, and yet he was terrified of letting his team down. So he decided to

PUT IN THE HOURS.

And finally there is the story of one of the most famous athletes of all time who won four Olympic gold medals in front of a world leader who not only wanted him to lose, but hated him because of the colour of his skin. He knew that when no one else does you have to

BELIEVE IN YOURSELF.

So whatever fear you are fighting to overcome, remember there will be a sports legend who has felt the same — and found a way to beat it.

LEGEND ID
ADAM
PEATY

BORN: 28 December 1994

NATIONALITY: British

SPORT: Swimming

LEGEND STATUS: Won the Olympic gold medal in 2016 in the 100 metres breaststroke. Set world records in the 50 and 100 metres breaststroke.

IN A DUSTY blue arena in Rio de Janeiro, Brazil, Adam Peaty stood on his block at the start of the 100 metres breaststroke final. This was the Olympic Games in 2016 and he had been waiting for this night for years. He was 21 and wanted to win gold.

There was a moment of hush as everyone waited for the starting gun. When it sounded, the crowd leapt to their feet as one. This was it. The noise sounded like a thunderstorm. In the press box, where I had my laptop open and had started a report for my newspaper, all the journalists stopped typing to watch the race.

I remember thinking that all those years of getting up for training at 4.30 a.m. every day before school had been reduced to less than one minute of Adam's life. If he lost, he would have another four years to wait for the next Olympic Games. That felt like a lifetime away. It was now or never.

But Adam wasn't in the lead. In the lane next to him his great South African rival, Cameron van der Burgh, was pulling ahead.

OH NO! WAS HE GOING TO BE BEATEN ON HIS BIG NIGHT?

I thought about Adam's coach, Mel Marshall, and what must be going through her head as she watched him from the side of the pool. She had been a world number one swimmer herself, years earlier, but had suffered a terrible setback when her nerves got to her and she failed to qualify for the Olympic final in Beijing, China, 2008.

She retired and became a coach. One day, she saw a fourteen-year-old boy named Adam at her local pool. She thought he had raw talent and was determined he wouldn't be beaten by his fear like she had. That was in 2009. Now here they were in Brazil for the 2016 Olympics.

Adam clawed back the distance between him and van der Burgh. When the swimmers turned at the halfway stage, Adam was in the lead. And then he began to extend further away from van der Burgh.

Commentators for all the different TV channels were watching from the seats next to me. The Brazilian commentator was so excited by what he was seeing that his face was getting redder and his voice was getting higher and louder. It looked like he might explode any second.

Adam touched the wall in front of him. He had won! The gold medal was his. His time was 57.13 seconds. The scoreboard flashed up:

NEW WORLD RECORD

★ ★ ★

I IMMEDIATELY LEFT my laptop and rushed down the stairs to the press area where the swimmers do interviews after their races.

Adam's family were already there. His dad had a Union Jack flag draped over his shoulders. His girlfriend gave Adam a home-made flapjack. Up until that night Adam was on a strict training diet and he was not allowed to eat any biscuits, sweets, crisps or cakes. It is not always easy being a legend.

As he tucked into the flapjack, he told me that before he dived into the pool, he had said three words to himself. They were:

"BURN THE BOATS!"

23

I asked him what that phrase meant. He said he had no time in the race to doubt himself. He knew that if he spent any energy thinking about his opponents, then it would be energy wasted. Fearing his rivals, like Cameron van der Burgh, might make him a millisecond slower. That could be the difference between winning and losing a gold medal.

Those words come from a story in history. In 1519, a Spanish general called Hernán Cortés sailed with his army to Mexico where he wanted to seize treasure. But some of Cortés's men were afraid. They did not think they could win a battle. They wanted to go home. So, legend has it, Hernán Cortés burnt his own boats.

WHAT! Sounds daft, doesn't it?

Historians have pointed out that Cortés was a brutal leader, but also a tactical genius. He burnt his own boats to make his men realize there was no turning back. They had no choice but to stay and fight. It made his own men more determined. Instead of wondering whether they should go home, they focused everything on the task in front of them. They won the treasure for Cortés.

Adam's story of overcoming his self-doubt to focus on the task in front of him is made even more amazing by another fact.

The greatest swimmer in the world used to be afraid of water.

The Olympic swimming champion was so scared of water that he would not even have a shower. "I didn't like going in water at all," he said. "I'd go to the pool with Mum and start climbing up her arm to get out." He only overcame his fear when he went swimming with a friend. He didn't want to make a scene, so his embarrassment got the better of his fear. Then he noticed that other kids were having fun. Slowly, he managed to change his behaviour.

Fear isn't something that you face once and then it goes away. It takes time and effort. When Adam started racing, he also had to learn to overcome his nerves. As he held his gold medal that night in Brazil he told us:

"When I was fourteen I hated racing in finals because I was so nervous. It's almost like you want to puke. You just think, 'I really don't want to do this'. But as soon as you get into the water training comes into play."

Then he said something that I thought was really interesting.

"You can't just train your body and not your mind."

We might not be able to train so that we can swim like Adam Peaty, but we can train our minds. Everyone has days where they face challenges and things don't go to plan. Everyone struggles. But Adam has trained himself not to give up on those days. He knows the situation probably isn't as bad as he thinks in that particular moment. He can face his fears and get through it.

You too can try to burn the boats by committing to something and giving it your all. Don't be afraid to believe in yourself, even on the tough days.

Not long after setting the world record, Adam and Mel came up with a new target. They called it Project 56.

The aim was for Adam to be the first man to swim 100 metres in under 57 seconds. People said it couldn't be done. That it was off the scale.

In June 2019, Adam clocked 56.88 seconds.

When I next met him, I asked him why he had got a tattoo of a big lion on his arm. He said:

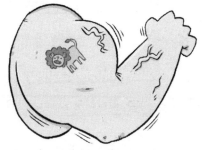

"NOBODY WANTS A SMALL LION, DO THEY?"

★ LEGEND LESSON ★

BURN YOUR BOATS.

Banish your doubts. Commit to something and put all your energy and focus into it.

LEGEND ID
SOPHIA FLÖRSCH

BORN: 1 December 2000

NATIONALITY: German

SPORT: Motor racing

LEGEND STATUS: First woman to race in the

Formula 3 Championship. Winner of the Laureus

World Comeback of the Year award. Has named

her cars Paul and Hugo.

THE GRANDSTANDS WERE packed at the famous racing track in Macau, China in 2018. Sophia Flörsch was roaring around the circuit at 171 mph in her dazzling black and orange Formula 3 car. She was seventeen and her dream was to become a famous racing driver. This was a chance to show everyone what she could do. She focused on the back of the car in front of her and prepared to slow down into the next corner. That's when she knew something was wrong.

Sophia had lost control of the left side of the car. She hit a kerb, another car and then realized she was in the air. She could smell the petrol and hear the roar of the engine. She did not hear the screams.

Her training for a crash situation kicked in. She took her hands off the steering wheel and braced herself. In that terrifying second, she knew she was going to hit something very hard. What she didn't know was that she was flying through the air

That's backwards.

Her car rocketed into some netting and then smashed into a hut where photographers had been taking pictures of the race. "It was like a missile coming at a million miles an hour," one said. He was lucky. One of the photographers had his jaw broken. Another was bleeding. But Sophia was in the most trouble of all.

The fire extinguisher in the car had gone off and there was foam in her eyes and mouth. Then she felt the terrible pain in her back.

Her dad, Alex, had been watching the race but had missed the crash. He rushed to the team room, where one of the crew was looking at a replay of the crash on his phone. When he saw Alex he threw his phone down and started crying. That was when Alex knew it was bad.

Then he received a text from Sophia's mother, who was watching from home in Munich, Germany. The message was simple.

"IS SHE ALIVE?"

Sophia was still conscious and had been lifted out of her car and stretchered to the hospital near the track. When Alex got there he was told Sophia had broken her spine. A bone splinter in her back was millimetres away from damaging her spinal cord and leaving her unable to walk again.

The operation to fix her broken back was meant to take two hours. The surgeons decided the safest way to get to the spine was to cut into the front of Sophia's neck. They had to be extremely careful because one slip might damage a nerve and leave her paralysed.

Eleven hours later, the team all breathed a sigh of relief. They had saved her.

31

TWO MONTHS LATER, I arranged to meet Sophia and Alex in Munich. I wanted to ask Sophia about the crash. I also wanted to know whether she would dare get back into a car and race again. She said:

"I was shocked when I watched the film of the crash because the video is horrible. In the car it felt different. If I watch it now it does not feel like me crashing. I watch it and think, 'This guy is not going to survive.'"

She was unable to move for five days after the surgery and she lost five kilograms of muscle. She was given so many painkillers that she saw pink elephants. But against the odds, she had survived. Then she got her phone back and realized she had

120,000 new Instagram followers.

Sophia said all she wanted to do now was go back to racing. So I asked her if she was afraid after what had happened to her in Macau.

She said she had thought about fate, but never about stopping racing. "The crash was one of the worst ones of recent years, but I survived. It proves the car is actually really safe."

Some people might have thought crashing backwards at 171 mph showed how dangerous racing was. For Sophia it did the opposite – surviving the crash actually showed her how safe it was. Whatever happened to her in the future, she now knew that she could handle it.

In between mouthfuls of lunch, Sophia told me how she had been handling problems for years. She had started racing go-karts when she was four. That was because she had fallen off a motorbike and hurt her arm so her dad thought four wheels would be safer!

But it had never been easy. The drivers Sophia was racing against were all boys. If Sophia beat them, they would make excuses rather than accept they had been beaten. Some boys would deliberately drive into her or pretend to break down because they thought it was embarrassing to lose to a girl. Sophia heard what the boys said and taught herself to handle it. She even saw their insults as a challenge.

Every challenge she faced made her more resilient. The same works for us. Every time we face our fears, we become stronger.

It took just 106 days for Sophia to get back in her Formula 3 car and start racing again. I called her up after her first race. She said:

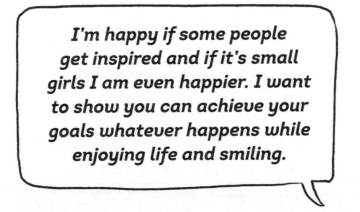

I'm happy if some people get inspired and if it's small girls I am even happier. I want to show you can achieve your goals whatever happens while enjoying life and smiling.

★ LEGEND LESSON ★

YOU CAN HANDLE IT.

Every challenge you face will build your resilience and enable you to handle your fears.

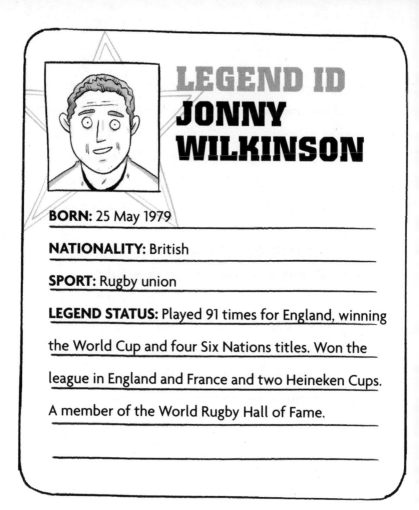

LEGEND ID
JONNY WILKINSON

BORN: 25 May 1979

NATIONALITY: British

SPORT: Rugby union

LEGEND STATUS: Played 91 times for England, winning the World Cup and four Six Nations titles. Won the league in England and France and two Heineken Cups. A member of the World Rugby Hall of Fame.

IT WAS THE final of the 2003 Rugby World Cup in Australia and Jonny Wilkinson was tired. The match had gone into extra time and England had been playing against a mighty Australia side on their own ground in Sydney for almost 100 minutes. Over the course of the tournament, Jonny had become the star of an England team trying to win their first World Cup trophy. He was wet from the rain and sweat. He knew his muscles would be screaming in pain the next day, but he did not care. The scores were level at 14–14. There were 82,597 people going wild in the stadium.

There was ONE minute of extra time left to play.

Jonny had missed three drop goals in the game. If any of them had gone over the bar, then England would have already won the cup. His biggest fear was that he would be seen as the reason his country lost.

England had been ahead 14–5 at half-time, but the Australians refused to give in. They fought their way back. Then Elton Flatley, the Australian number 10, kicked a penalty to level the score and take the final to extra time. It had been a crushing blow to England.

40 SECONDS LEFT...

Now extra time was almost over. Matt Dawson, one of Jonny's team mates, had the ball and spotted a small gap. He wriggled through it and ran towards the Australia try line. Four Australia players hammered him to the ground. The giant England captain, Martin Johnson, then picked up the ball and battered his way forward before he was tackled. Jonny knew this was his moment. The ball was coming back to him with the next pass. He got in position to kick a drop goal.

26 SECONDS LEFT...

Dawson passed back to Jonny. Normally Jonny kicked with his left foot. But the angle of the pass meant this time he would have to use his right. This was it. All or nothing.

In the press box, the journalists and TV commentators couldn't believe what they were seeing. The stakes for the next few seconds couldn't be higher. Ian Robertson, who was commentating for the BBC, couldn't keep the excitement out of his voice. As Jonny pulled his right leg back and let the ball fall towards the ground, millions of people watching in England and all around the world held their breath. Robertson said:

"HE DROPS FOR WORLD CUP GLORY!"

The ball sailed between the posts. England were ahead! Jonny felt like he was in a dream. It was almost as if someone else had just kicked that goal. He had been training for this moment ever since he started playing rugby. He half-celebrated, but realized there was still just enough time for Australia to kick off. If Australia won the ball back they would still have a chance.

There was pandemonium on the touchline and in the stands. From the kick-off an England player caught the ball. Mike Catt turned and booted the ball out of play to end the match. England were the World Cup champions and Jonny, with that winning kick, was a superstar.

★ ★ ★

SINCE THAT INCREDIBLE final in 2003 I have interviewed Jonny lots of times. What I found remarkable was that he admitted he was scared of playing rugby. He used to enjoy it when he was younger, but as he got better something changed.

"I used to dread coming into the England camp before matches. The reason was the pressure and the scrutiny. I couldn't handle the fact someone might not think I was good enough."

He still felt like this when he was winning the World Cup and scoring a record 1,179 points for England.

People saw Jonny and thought life was easy for him. He was brilliant. He could kick goals with both feet. He was strong. People liked him. He was the BBC Sports Personality of the Year. But he had fears just like you or me.

Jonny never wanted to let anyone down. Once we met at a rugby ground before the 2015 World Cup in England. He sat in the changing room and said to me:

"The responsibility as England's kicker scared me."

41

Lots of matches were very close and the kicker was often the player who decided the outcome. Jonny would be worried sick that all the others players' hard work would count for nothing if he fluffed a kick. He felt the strain of thinking people would forget all the good things he did and only remember the missed kicks.

His way of dealing with his fear was to practise as hard as he could. He figured that if he trained harder than other players, he had a better chance of winning matches and not letting anyone down. On some days he would kick the ball for seven hours without looking at his watch.

After every training session, he set himself a challenge of kicking six penalties in a row before he would let himself go home. Normally this didn't take him long, but sometimes it could take an extra 90 minutes. Sometimes it was dark when he left.

Never be fooled into thinking success is effortless. You might think rugby comes easily to Jonny or football comes easily to Cristiano Ronaldo but they train harder than anyone.

One famous writer once said it takes 10,000 hours of practice to become fantastic at anything. Some people think it takes more. Others think it takes less. What we know for sure is that you will feel more in control and less afraid of a situation if you have done as much preparation as possible.

Jonny always had his fears but he knew that if he had kicked thousands of drop goals in training then he would be more confident when it really mattered.

And with 26 seconds to go in the World Cup final it really, really mattered.

★ LEGEND LESSON ★

PUT IN THE HOURS.

Even the most talented sports legends have fears, but practice and preparation can help you overcome them.

LEGEND ID
JESSE OWENS

BORN: 12 September 1913

DIED: 31 March 1980

NATIONALITY: American

SPORT: Athletics

LEGEND STATUS: Won four gold medals in seven days at the 1936 Olympic Games. Set five world records and equalled a sixth in 45 minutes.

JESSE OWENS KNELT on the starting line of the 100 metres final at the Olympic Games in Berlin, Germany. The year was 1936. Ralph Metcalfe, his great USA rival, was next to him, but Jesse had bigger things to worry about. Adolf Hitler, the leader of Nazi Germany, was watching the final. Hitler was using the Olympics to show off his Nazi regime. He believed in a master race of people with blond hair and blue eyes. He openly discriminated against minority groups including Jewish and Black people. Jesse, who was a Black man, looked down the track and concentrated. He thought:

BELIEVE IN YOURSELF.

Hitler thought the German athletes, who embodied his beliefs, would win gold and prove he was right. Jesse was not the only Black athlete at the Olympics, but he was the best. Jesse knew that Hitler was wrong and that the stakes were high. This was a race for all minority groups.

Jesse got off to a FLYING start.

He was in the lead, but he didn't know by how much because he could not waste time by looking behind. Ralph always finished strongly. He heard footsteps close behind him as he crossed the line in

10.3 SECONDS.

Ralph finished in 10.4 seconds. Jesse had won by a tenth of a second.

THAT'S NOT EVEN A SNEEZE.

Hitler did not shake Jesse's hand afterwards. He was furious that Black athletes were triumphing at his Olympics. Jesse went on to win three more gold medals that week – in the 200 metres, the long jump and the relay. He became the first American track and field athlete to win four gold medals at a single Olympic Games. He was the star of Hitler's show.

★ ★ ★

THIS HAPPENED NOT far off 100 years ago. Jesse died in 1980, but is still one of the most famous sportspeople in America. I have always been fascinated by what he achieved and the courage he displayed in 1936. Over the years I have interviewed some of his daughters and grandchildren to find out more about him. It was from them that I heard the incredible story of what happened the day after the 100 metres final.

It was the qualifying round for the long jump. Every athlete had three jumps to hit a certain distance and make the final. Still wearing his tracksuit, Jesse took a practice jump, but the German officials counted it as one of his goes. Jesse had just been warming up and he complained, but they would not change their minds. Then he messed up his second jump, leaving him with only one chance left to make the final. He started to panic.

Legend has it that this is when a German long jumper came up to Jesse. He was tall, with blond hair and blue eyes, and looked like Hitler's perfect athlete. He said his name was Luz Long and he wanted to help Jesse. This was a dangerous thing for a German to do, with Hitler watching and hoping Jesse would fail. Luz told Jesse that he should change his take-off point. He left a towel by the track and said Jesse must jump when he reached it. Jesse did just that and qualified for the final.

That final was fantastic. Each man had six jumps and the one who went the furthest would get the gold medal. Jesse set a new Olympic record when he jumped 7.87 metres.

THAT'S LONGER THAN YOUR CLASSROOM!

Luz was not finished yet, though, and he equalled it. But Jesse was more confident now thanks to Luz's advice and he produced an even longer jump of 8.09 metres to set a new Olympic record and win the gold medal.

The first person to congratulate him, right in front of Hitler, was Luz. Luz was one of the big hopes for Germany,

but he had been beaten by a Black man. Hitler was furious that his beliefs in a master race had been shown to be false. Lots of high-ranking German soldiers in the stadium had all seen Luz help Jesse and then congratulate him, so both had good reason to be scared. The crowd were cheering for Jesse and Hitler was so unpredictable that who could tell how he would react?

Jesse had always faced prejudice and racism. This continued when he returned home to America as an Olympic hero. His daughter, Marlene Owens Rankin, would tell me how President Franklin D Roosevelt refused to invite him to the White House. Jesse was actually held in higher regard in Europe than at home. "He was admired by the Black community in the USA, but given the racial divisions it was not as open-armed," she said.

The story did not end there. Jesse and Luz continued to write to each other after the Olympics. When Hitler took Germany into the Second World War in 1939 Luz had no choice but to join up. He became a soldier fighting against America. The last letter he sent to Jesse said:

"My heart tells me this will be the last letter I write. If it is so I ask you something. It is for you to go to Germany when this war is done, some day find my son and tell him about his father. Tell him Jesse ... how things can be between men on this earth."

Not long afterwards Luz was killed in the war. But Jesse did find Luz's son and told him how brave Luz had been to defy Hitler in Berlin. Like Jesse, Luz knew the most important thing was to be true to yourself and not to let your fears hold you back from doing what you believed to be right. That is a lesson we can all learn from.

In 2009, the World Athletics Championships were held in the same stadium in Berlin, 73 years after Jesse had won four gold medals in seven days. His granddaughter, Marlene, went to Germany and met Luz's son, Kai. They presented the medals after the long jump final.

Marlene told me how her famous grandfather had managed to focus all those years ago:

"He did what he came to do and he did not let any outside forces change who he was."

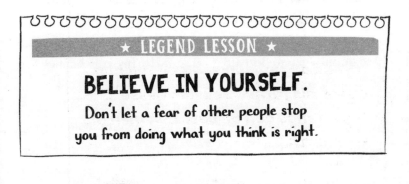

★ LEGEND LESSON ★

BELIEVE IN YOURSELF.

Don't let a fear of other people stop you from doing what you think is right.

LEGEND HEADLINES:

SURFING

Bethany Hamilton was thirteen when she went for her morning surf in Hawaii in 2003. She did not see the four-metre long tiger shark until it was too late. It bit off her left arm. Her friends helped her to paddle to the shore and tried to stop the bleeding with a rough bandage. Bethany was rushed to hospital, but the doctors were worried because, as well as her arm, she had lost more than half her blood. After a long operation she survived. One month later, Bethany faced her fears and got back on her surfboard. She then went on to win lots of big surfing competitions.

INVICTUS GAMES

Paul Vice was a soldier in the Royal Marines. When he was on patrol in Afghanistan a bomb went off. It left him with 400 different wounds. "It felt like my skin was on fire," he said. One of Paul's legs had to be amputated. He got the Military Cross for bravery but feared for his future without his job. He thought he wouldn't be able to do any physical activity again, but after he got an artificial leg he started playing lots of different sports. He went on to win seven medals at the 2016 Invictus Games for wounded soldiers and then started racing cars. He even climbed Mount Kilimanjaro. "Tell me I can't do something and I'll show you I can," he said to me.

FACING FEARS

TENNIS

Monica Seles was a superstar by the time she was sixteen when she became the youngest winner of the French Open in Paris in 1990. But her career took a shocking turn three years later when a man jumped out of the crowd at a match in Germany and stabbed her in the back. Monica recovered physically but the attack had a serious impact on her confidence. She feared going back to tennis in case someone else attacked her. Finally, after two years away, she made a courageous comeback. The following year she won the Australian Open.

RUGBY

Many people thought **Siya Kolisi**, the Black captain of the South African team for the 2019 Rugby World Cup, should not be in the team. For many years, South Africa had been divided on racial lines, with white people having all the power. Siya was born in a poor township. He suffered racism and jealousy as he rose to the top of rugby, but he overcame all his fears about not fitting in through determination. Against all the odds, South Africa won the World Cup against England in 2019 and Siya became the first Black man to lift the trophy as the winning captain.

CHAPTER 2:
OVERCOMING FAILURE

Here is another question. What is failure?

That's an easy one to answer, isn't it? Failure is messing up a test or losing a match or forgetting to put your trousers on in the morning.

WRONG!

Albert Einstein was a very famous scientist. He is widely considered to have been a genius. And yet he could not talk until he was four. Nobody thought he was very clever at that point. He lived his life by the following saying:

Failure is success in progress.

What he meant was that if you are going to succeed at anything then you have to make mistakes. Nobody gets on a bike for the first time and rides it perfectly. You have to fall off first. Maybe you'll even crash into a lamp post.

Nobody *wants* to fail because it can make us feel daft. But if we remember that everybody fails at some point in their lives then it makes it easier to deal with. What matters is what you do after you fail.

Imagine that you are a basketball player in the NBA, the biggest league in the world. And now imagine

you miss 9,000 shots.

That is a lot of failure. You might expect to get kicked off the team for that. But that is how many shots Michael Jordan says he missed during his NBA career. And he is the most famous basketball player in history. Every year his team, the Chicago Bulls, paid him £33 million.

Why did they do that if he missed 9,000 shots?

He also scored 32,292 points.

Michael Jordan said he was so good at scoring because he was not afraid to miss.

"I've failed over and over again in my life which is why I succeed."

He "failed" 9,000 times and nobody remembers any of them. Failure was success in progress.

Watching sport all over the world has taught me a lot about failure – or at least what we think is failure. For a start, in sport, there are a lot more losers than winners. But does losing always mean failure?

Take the Wimbledon tennis championships. There are 256 players in the first round of the men's and women's singles but only one winner in each. Would you call the other 254 people who played at the most famous tennis tournament in the world *failures*?

Or how about Sergio Parisse, one of the world's greatest rugby players. He has lost 106 international games. That is more than any other player in the world, but nobody thinks the Italian rugby legend is a loser.

Jack Green considered himself a failure when he fell over in front of 80,000 people in the semi-finals of the 400 metre hurdles at the 2012 Olympics in London. But do you know how many people get to the Olympics?

One in every 780,000 people.

Jack realized it was a brilliant achievement to even get to the Olympics. He stopped judging himself against other people. He told me the best way to improve is to:

"Compare yourself to yesterday's you."

We need to change the way we look at failure if we are to reach our potential. What matters most is how we react when things do not go as planned. Sometimes that means we have to be like Jack and reframe failure.

What that means is failure does not define you. If you lose a match, *you* are not a loser. You just lost a match. That experience is actually a building block on the way to winning the next one.

So how do our sports legends deal with failure? How do they keep going when everything seems to be going wrong? I wanted to find out the answers.

In this chapter, we will meet the Olympic 400 metres sprinter whose dream ended when he got injured during the biggest race of his life. What happened next made him even more famous and showed

IT'S NOT JUST ABOUT WINNING AND LOSING.

Then there is the brilliant heavyweight boxer who suffered a huge embarrassment when he lost a fight to a supposed no-hoper. He won back his titles because you have to

LEARN FROM YOUR MISTAKES.

We meet one of athletics' biggest stars who felt she did not belong at the top and had no confidence. She bounced back spectacularly after realizing

HAPPINESS COMES FROM INSIDE.

And then there is the record-breaking cyclist. She felt she had let everyone down, but when she was cut and bruised after a terrible crash her reaction was to

GET BACK ON THE BIKE.

Remember that if you learn from a mistake then it is not a failure. It is actually really useful. It means you will do better next time.

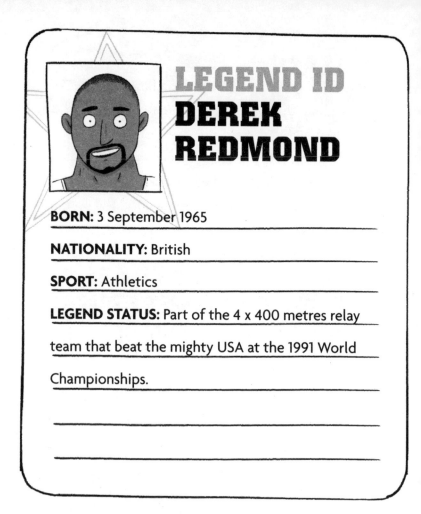

LEGEND ID
DEREK REDMOND

BORN: 3 September 1965

NATIONALITY: British

SPORT: Athletics

LEGEND STATUS: Part of the 4 x 400 metres relay team that beat the mighty USA at the 1991 World Championships.

DEREK REDMOND WAS feeling good. It was the start of the 400 metres semi-final at the 1992 Olympic Games in Barcelona, Spain. He had been the fastest man in the first round and he was in the shape of his life. In his heart he was sure that he was going to win the gold medal and become

Olympic champion. It was everything he had dreamt of.

He had no idea that the next minute would make him famous around the world … for finishing last!

Derek was in lane five. He got off to a good start. He went around the first bend feeling comfortable. He had suffered lots of injuries over the past few years and had had sixteen operations. Now he was finally running pain-free. He tore down the back straight, listening to the crowd cheer.

"I wasn't even breaking sweat."

Then Derek's race suddenly changed. After 150 metres, he felt a terrible pain in the back of his right thigh. He hobbled to a stop. The other seven runners raced away from him. Derek bent down on his left knee and began to cry.

"The disbelief, I can't tell you, I went into denial and hit the floor."

The hamstring muscle in his thigh had snapped. That should have been the end of Derek's race. But instead Derek did something extraordinary. The agony was awful, but as he saw the medical staff at the side of the track, he said to himself:

"There's no way I'm leaving the Olympics on a stretcher."

Derek decided he was going to finish the race. So even though all the other runners had now crossed the finishing line and he could only use his uninjured leg, Derek got up and carried on.

He started with a hop. A grimace spread across his face. Even from the grandstands people could tell that he was crying. Derek told himself he was going to get to that line if it was the last thing he did. And, as the crowd realized what was happening, they began to cheer.

That was when an older man in shorts and a baseball cap jumped a barrier and ran onto the track. Security guards tried to stop him, but he pushed them away and headed directly for Derek.

IT WAS HIS DAD.

Jim let Derek rest his head on his shoulder and supported one of his hands. Seeing the distress on his son's face Jim said:

"You don't need to do this."

But Derek did. They were in this together and they inched their way towards the finishing line.

Step by step, the pain grew worse and the noise grew louder. Nobody was looking at Steve Lewis, the American who had won the race. They were too mesmerized by this man struggling through pain to achieve last place.

Finally they got to the finish. Instead of a gold medal, Derek was a distant last.

Derek was angry because his Olympic dream was over. He would have to wait another four years for another go, and by then he would not be as fast.

He also felt like he had failed. Interestingly, he was the only person who thought so.

The photograph of Derek and Jim made the front page of newspapers all over the world. Journalists wanted to interview both him and Jim. Jim told them:

**"I'm the proudest father alive.
I'm prouder of him than I would have
been if he had won the gold medal. It took
a lot of guts for him to do what he did."**

★ ★ ★

MANY YEARS LATER I got to meet Derek. We were at a motorcycle race together where Derek was now running a team. We sat down by the pit lane as the bikers revved their engines and he told me it took him a long time to see his "failure" the same way other people did. He had got up off the ground because he thought he might be able to catch the rest of the runners up. But then he realized they had all finished.

"That was like someone plunging a knife into me. I felt stubbornness, disappointment and annoyance. I said to myself, 'I'm going to finish this race'. Then my dad arrived. I said, 'Get me back in my lane'. I remember saying, 'Why me? Why me? What have I done to deserve this?'"

He told me that to start with he could not understand why people were so interested in the way he handled the situation.

"I got angry and shut myself off. But then something clicked."

He understood that he hadn't failed just because he hadn't won. He thought about all the messages he had received from people he didn't even know. One was from a Canadian athlete. It said:

"Long after the names of the medallists have faded from our minds you will be remembered for having finished, for having tried so hard, for having a father demonstrate the strength of his love for his son."

Derek's life would have been different in other ways too. Sharron Davies, an Olympic swimmer, had been so impressed by his bravery that she had found him after the race to congratulate him. It was an important meeting, because they ended up getting married.

Derek discovered the most important thing was not that he lost, but *how* he lost. Feeling sorry for ourselves when things don't go our way often doesn't do us any good – especially if what went wrong was something out of our control, like an injury. It would be nice to be able to control everything, but random things happen. All you can do is react in the most positive way to any setback.

If Derek had quit and left the stadium on a stretcher it would not have changed the result of the race. But by getting up he proved to himself – and the rest of the world – that he had courage and resilience. When we are brave and keep going, we get a sense of pride from whatever we achieve. It's not all about winning.

There were 260 gold medals won at the 1992 Olympic Games. That Canadian athlete was right. Most of the winners have been forgotten but everybody remembers Derek Redmond. He has given inspirational talks all over the world and tells people the same thing: keep going.

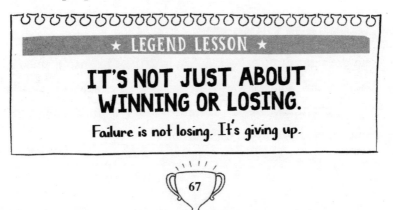

★ LEGEND LESSON ★

IT'S NOT JUST ABOUT WINNING OR LOSING.

Failure is not losing. It's giving up.

LEGEND ID
ANTHONY JOSHUA

BORN: 15 October 1989

NATIONALITY: British

SPORT: Boxing

LEGEND STATUS: Won a gold medal at the 2012 Olympics. Then won the heavyweight world title – twice. His fights attract crowds of 95,000 people.

EVERYBODY THOUGHT Anthony Joshua was going to win the fight in New York, USA, in 2019. The man from London, the "king of the world", was the heavyweight boxing champion and he had never lost. For his last four fights he had been paid the sum of

£50 million.

This time, he was up against a little-known American challenger called Andy Ruiz with four different world title belts on the line. Ruiz did not have the muscular physique of a boxer. Over the past few days people had called him "a fat slob", a "chubby kid" and worse. Chicken and pizza were Andy's favourites and he always had two Snickers bars before a fight. No one thought he had a chance.

Inside the famous Madison Square Garden arena, you could taste the anticipation. Fans cheered and then booed as images of Anthony and Andy flashed up on the giant TV screen above the ring. The smell from the hotdog stall drifted over our seats. The fans who had travelled from the UK were not expecting to be staying for long. Most people predicted that AJ, as everyone called Anthony, would win in two rounds. There was a buzz of excitement as the fighters made their way to the ring.

But the first two rounds showed Andy was much better than expected. He was fast and strong. I was sitting at the ringside with the other journalists and I could see he had the word **VICTORIOUS** tattooed across his back.

Then came the sensational third round.

AJ threw his left hand and Andy fell to the canvas hurt.
We started to type our stories for the newspapers. It looked
like it was all over. But then Andy got off the floor and went
on the attack. And he stunned thousands of fans when he
knocked AJ down. Wearily, AJ got back up. He was dazed. In
all his training he had not planned for this. Towards the end
of the round he was almost knocked out of the ring. He was
gasping for air now.

The bell rang for the end of the round. AJ knew he
was in danger as he sat down on his stool in his corner. He
knew all the kids back at his old gym in London would

be watching on TV. They would be devastated if he lost. He tried as hard as he could to carry on. He made it to the seventh round before the referee stopped the fight and declared Andy the winner.

"WOW!"

was all the TV commentator sitting in front of me could say. He had been left speechless. It suddenly dawned on everyone that the "chubby kid" was the champion!

We journalists were stunned too. "I can't believe what I've just seen," one of my friends said to me.

★ ★ ★

I FELT SORRY for AJ but I was pleased for Andy. I had spoken to Andy a few days before and he told me how people used to make fun of him at school because he was overweight. He said:

"I'm fighting for all the misfits."

Andy knew it doesn't matter what shape or size you are, it is what's inside that counts.

After the boxers had taken a shower and got changed, it was time for the press conference. AJ came into the room and did something very rare and really impressive. From interviewing sportspeople, I knew that they often make excuses when things go wrong. They blame:

THE REFEREE

BAD LUCK —

CHEATING

INJURY

AJ was crushed and disappointed, but he told us the honest truth.

The better man won.

It was a big thing to say. Already on social media people were making fun of AJ. Other boxers were saying he had never really been very good and that he had been lucky in his past fights. But still AJ managed to put on a brave face and congratulate Andy.

And then he set about beating him in the rematch.

★ ★ ★

THAT CAME SIX months later. Andy enjoyed his success. He bought his mum a new house and he ate lots of free Snickers.

It was a harder time for AJ. People wondered if his career was finished. He got called lots of names.

But AJ had faced challenges before. When he was young he had been in trouble with the police. He had to wear an electronic tag on his leg so they knew where he was. He had used sport to turn his life round, by getting fit and becoming disciplined. He was grateful for having a second chance and had learnt his lesson.

Now he had to learn from his defeat by Andy.

AJ knew you had to give your very best to every situation. Nothing worthwhile comes easily. He also knew you should not judge people by how they look. To his cost, AJ had underestimated Andy.

He went home and studied the first fight with his trainer, Rob McCracken. They came up with a plan to win back the title.

They knew AJ had longer arms, so they decided he should stand further away from Andy and use that reach to score points. AJ now knew just how hard Andy could punch, so he would jab away at him from a distance and stop him getting close. The second part of the plan involved AJ losing weight so he could move out of Andy's way faster.

"I had to learn but I never lost heart."

Instead of wasting time and emotion by feeling sorry for himself AJ learnt from his failure and came back stronger. He looked at what he had done wrong both before the fight and during it. He analysed the problem and came up with a solution. If you fail at something, don't beat yourself up about it. Think about what you did wrong and how you can stop it happening again. Ask what you can learn from it.

AJ's plan worked. Six months later, in a desert city in Saudi Arabia, he walked out into the ring and beat Andy in the rematch. AJ boxed to his plan and won easily on points after twelve rounds. He was the

KING OF THE WORLD AGAIN.

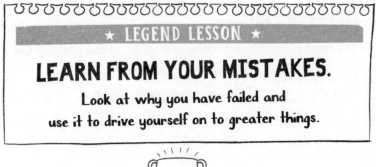

★ LEGEND LESSON ★

LEARN FROM YOUR MISTAKES.

Look at why you have failed and
use it to drive yourself on to greater things.

LEGEND ID

KATARINA JOHNSON-THOMPSON

BORN: 9 January 1993

NATIONALITY: British

SPORT: Athletics

LEGEND STATUS: Won the world heptathlon title in 2019 and set a British record. Also won the Commonwealth Games gold medal and world indoor titles in 2018.

FOR YEARS SOME people said Katarina Johnson-Thompson had been getting it wrong on the big stage. It did not help that what she did was incredibly difficult. The heptathlon is made up of seven different events so Kat had to be good at:

HIGH JUMP

100 METRES HURDLES

SHOT-PUT

200 METRES

LONG JUMP

JAVELIN

800 METRES

In the heptathlon you get points for your performance in each event and the athlete who has the most points at the end is the winner. At the 2016 Olympic Games in Rio de Janeiro, Brazil, it was the long jump and shot-put that had let Kat down. She came sixth. The year after, at the 2017 World Championships in London, she was fifth. Now it was 2019 and she was back at the World Championships in Qatar. This time she was facing Belgium's Nafi Thiam – the Olympic champion who people were saying was the greatest heptathlete of all time.

When I interviewed Kat before the competition, she admitted she suffered from something called

IMPOSTER SYNDROME.

Even though she had won lots of medals, including the European indoor title a few months earlier, she still struggled with her self-confidence. She felt like she was playing a part and that she was a fake. She didn't think she belonged in the big championships because she didn't think she was good enough. I thought it was amazing that such a talented sports star struggled so much to believe in herself.

Kat had even wondered about quitting the heptathlon. She was a good high jumper so she could just compete in that without the other six events. It would be a lot easier. When she finished two days of gruelling competition in the heptathlon she would have to get in a wheelie bin full of ice-cold water to soothe her aches and pains. It was an event that hurt.

But Kat had decided she had more to give and so she refused to quit. She is a big fan of Liverpool FC and she remembered how they had come back from 3–0 down in the Champions League Final in 2005 (this incredible match is covered later in *Sports Legends*).

She moved to France, where she had no friends, so that she would not be distracted. She got a new coach and began to work on her weaknesses.

In Qatar for the 2019 World Championships it was boiling hot, so there were giant blowers to keep the athletes cool. Despite that Kat was feeling the heat. The pressure was on. For lots of people, including myself, the highlight of the whole championships came down to

The journalists' seats were right by the finishing line.
I felt lucky to be there with such a good view. When a race
finished, you could see the sweat pouring off the athletes.
Some crossed the line and cried because their races had
gone wrong. Others were smiling through their tiredness.
I saw one athlete throw up.

I looked back down the track to where Kat was lining
up at the start of her first event. I felt nervous for her.

But right from the start Kat looked at the top of her
game. She ran her fastest-ever hurdles time and produced
her best-ever shot-put to lead Thiam by 96 points after the
first day of competition. That sounds a lot but Thiam's best
events – the long jump and javelin – came on the second
day. It might not be enough.

When they returned the next day, Kat was not in the
mood to let her lead slip. Her long jump of 6.77 metres was
good and then she launched the javelin high into the night.
When that landed she knew she was almost home. There
was only the 800 metres left.

She ran brilliantly and then collapsed in exhaustion at
the side of the track next to Thiam. She knew she had won
before all the points were added up from the seven events.
From feeling like she did not belong at the very top Kat was
now the world champion and the British record holder. She

had put all seven pieces of her jigsaw together and scored an incredible

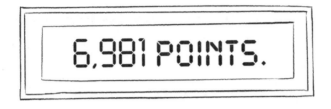

6,981 POINTS.

Kat and Thiam were arch-rivals, but when I looked over, I saw them talking to each other. They were draped in the flags of their countries, but they obviously respected each other and their sport.

★ ★ ★

THE NEXT MORNING, a few journalists, including myself, went to see Kat at the British team hotel. We sat down in an empty restaurant and she explained how she had got over her past failures. She said:

"The low moments have helped me."

All the setbacks had made her moment of triumph all the sweeter.

> *After the last two World Championships I went back to my hotel room and cried and cried for hours. This time they were tears of joy.*

She admitted she had started to hate sport. She had lost the enjoyment she used to get from it. Part of that was because of all the injuries that led to poor results. She also had people calling her a failure.

Talking about facing criticism, she said: "I didn't go looking for it but it comes from everywhere. It wasn't just Twitter, but questions from people everywhere."

I asked her how close she had come to quitting when it went wrong at the Olympics three years earlier. Her eyes welled up with tears. She excused herself and left the room for a minute. When she came back she explained it was just so hard to think back to how much of a failure she had felt a few years ago.

Now she realized you can't worry about what other people think about you. And she couldn't worry about Thiam either. "I learnt that you just can't pin happiness on external things," she said.

"You have to find it within yourself."

She meant you can't control what other people think about you or the things they do. It's the same for everyone. With social media, it is easy to worry about how many likes or shares or reposts we get online. But we cannot control that and it is giving power to other people.

We can only control what we think.

Kat did not worry about being an imposter any more. She had hit rock bottom and bounced back and found her own happiness on her own terms. A famous runner called Michael Johnson put it best. He said Kat had slayed her dragons.

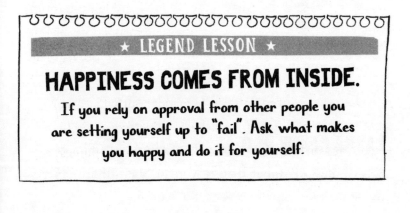

★ LEGEND LESSON ★

HAPPINESS COMES FROM INSIDE.

If you rely on approval from other people you are setting yourself up to "fail". Ask what makes you happy and do it for yourself.

LEGEND ID
LAURA KENNY

BORN: 24 April 1992

NATIONALITY: British

SPORT: Track cycling

LEGEND STATUS: Great Britain's most successful female Olympian. Won four Olympic gold medals (two in 2012 and two in 2016), as well as seven World Championship titles and fourteen European gold medals.

LAURA KENNY HAD already got more Olympic gold medals than any other British woman. She had four. Her husband, Jason, also a track cyclist, had six.

THAT'S TEN GOLD MEDALS IN ONE HOUSE!

But Laura had taken time out of cycling to have baby Albie in 2017. When she came back she had to make do with a silver medal at the World Championships in 2019. That sounds great, but she was so used to winning she wasn't happy with the result. Now she was back at the World Championships in Berlin in 2020 and she was determined to prove she was still the best in the world.

Laura faced an additional challenge though. Track cycling is a dangerous sport. The circuit is called a velodrome and is made of hard wood. It has steep banks sloping to the centre. A few weeks earlier, Laura had crashed in a race and broken her shoulder. She could still feel the pain. But she ignored the injury as she prepared for the World Championships.

Her event involved four separate races. As the first race got to the final stages, she was in the pack of riders behind the leaders. She began to push harder. All around her, riders were racing at high speed within centimetres of each other.

With one lap to go, disaster struck!

It was so quick that she was on the floor before she knew what had happened. The rider in front of her fell and Laura could not avoid her. She crashed and slid along the wooden track. Then the rider behind her ran over Laura's legs. She began to slide down the banked corner. Then another rider hit her and went head over heels.

Laura finally came to a stop on the inside of the track. She held her head. Bikes were scattered on the floor. It had been a bad crash and her first thought was for her injured shoulder. She had been advised to have an operation on it. But that would have meant months away to recover and she wanted to race. She couldn't risk damaging it any more.

She spent a few seconds lying on the floor. The doctor rushed towards her. Her shoulder did not feel too bad, but then Laura could feel something wet around her eye. She suddenly realized blood was gushing from a new wound. She took off her helmet. The doctor told her to stay still and he dabbed at the gash with a cloth. Then he led her away to the medical centre.

Laura needed to have stitches. She had a terrible black eye and looked like she had been boxing rather than cycling. Most people would have quit there and then. But Laura was made of strong stuff. She was small, she had long pigtails and

SHE WAS A FIGHTER.

To stunned disbelief around the arena Laura returned just two hours later. We knew she was tough because you have to be to win all those gold medals, but this was something else. She looked terrible and probably felt it too. Her eye was swollen and purple, but Laura was determined to carry on. She had three races to go and she had not left baby Albie at home and come all this way to Germany to quit now.

She came twelfth in the end but many fans thought she was the true winner.

★ ★ ★

I HAD WATCHED that race on TV and I interviewed Laura not long afterwards on the telephone. She explained that she had felt she had let the team down the year before when she came second. That was why she hadn't wanted to give up this time. She talked about what happened in 2019 and said: "You might think a silver medal is great, but in my head it was only a negative."

She was coming back from what she thought was a failure. Her attitude was that if something went wrong then you had to put it behind you and get back on the bike.

"I should probably stop headbutting the floor shouldn't I?" she added.

It was a joke but Laura had already learnt her lesson. She said the crash was her fault because she had been in the middle of the pack of riders. Normally, she would go to the front to stay out of trouble. Then she would trust her speed and endurance to stop the others catching her. This time she was too cautious because of her damaged shoulder. She would not be cautious again.

When you have won as many gold medals as Laura,

you expect to finish higher than twelfth. By her very high standards it was a failure. But there is a thing called

CONTEXT.

What does that mean? Well, imagine you play in a football team and you lose 3–0 to the worst side in the entire world. That would be a disaster, right? Then imagine your team lose 3–0 to Manchester City. The score is the same but that would be a far better result.

This is context.

Laura came twelfth, but the context was that she was riding with an injured shoulder and had stitches and a black eye. She thought she had failed, but she carried on to make sure she got something positive from a bad day.

This is important. Nobody wins all the time. Everybody suffers bad days. From speaking to sports legends, I have found that the way they react to failure is what makes them successful.

Laura refused to quit. That is what we should all do when we make a mistake or think we have failed at something. Acknowledge the context,

THEN JUST GET BACK ON THE BIKE.

★ LEGEND LESSON ★

GET BACK ON THE BIKE.
If you think you have "failed" consider the context and find a positive.

LEGEND HEADLINES:

SWIMMING

Michael Phelps has won 23 Olympic gold medals. That is a huge number, but the American legend did not like swimming to start with. You might think that the first time he touched the pool, he turned into a dolphin, but no. "I was scared to put my face in the water," he admitted. He screamed and threw his goggles around! Rather than think he had failed at swimming, he committed himself to the sport. Then he found that swimming actually slowed his mind down and made him feel in control. He is now regarded as the greatest swimmer of all time.

ATHLETICS

Lolo Jones was the favourite to win gold in the 100 metre hurdles at the 2008 Olympics. She was well ahead in the final when she clipped the second to last hurdle and stumbled. She lost ground and finished seventh. "Why, why, why?" she asked. Lolo said stumbling like that happened twice a year. "It just happened to be in the biggest race of my life!" But she did not give up. She learnt from the mistake and became the world indoor champion two years later. Then she reset her goals and became part of the USA bobsleigh team at the 2014 Winter Olympics.

OVERCOMING FAILURE

BASKETBALL

In the 2016 NBA play-offs, Cleveland Cavaliers faced the mighty Golden State Warriors, in the best-of-seven final. **LeBron James** was the Cavaliers' star player but he could not stop the Warriors going 3–1 up. That meant LeBron and his teammates had to win the next three games. LeBron scored 41 points in the next two games to tie the series. In the last game, he produced a stunning defensive move that became known as "the block". Cleveland won their first championship. "The best teacher in life is experience," he said. "I ask myself, 'How do I learn from this loss?'"

FOOTBALL

In October 2019, **Southampton** lost 9–0 at home to Leicester City. This equalled the worst defeat ever in the top division of English football. Everybody expected the manager, Ralph Hasenhüttl, to lose his job. But the Austrian was given a chance and he worked tirelessly to make his team better. He reminded his players that they were good and that the match was a one-off and they could learn from it. They did. Southampton went on one of the best runs in the Premier League after that. Two months later they played Leicester again. This time they won 2–1.

CHAPTER 3:
DARE TO BE DIFFERENT

Do you want to fit in or do you want to stand out?

Most of us like to fit in with the people around us. We don't like the idea that we might be different. We want to be part of the in-crowd.

But what's so great about being ordinary? What I've discovered in sport is that it is often the people who dare to be different who become legends.

Take the story of a young Black boxer named Cassius Clay. When he was growing up in the 1950s, Black people in America were treated very badly. There were different areas for Black and white people to sit in restaurants and on buses. Black children were not allowed to go to the same schools as white children.

Black sports stars were expected to be grateful that they were allowed to compete at all. And then along came Cassius Clay.

He was different to any boxer who had come before. He was loud and funny. He made up poems about his opponents. He said:

"Float like a butterfly, sting like a bee, his hands can't hit what his eyes don't see."

On another occasion he said he was so mean that he made medicine sick. And he once boasted: "It's hard to be humble when you're as great as I am."

In the 1960s, Cassius Clay became the heavyweight boxing champion of the world.

After he won the world title he continued to behave as he wanted, not how other people expected him to. He refused to join the American army, because he did not agree with the war they were fighting in Vietnam. He was banned from boxing for three years because of that. Then he converted to Islam and changed his name to Muhammad Ali, which upset some people. Still he kept on boasting and showing his sense of humour.

When he was allowed to box again after his ban, he hadn't changed. He was still different to everyone else and still the best.

Muhammad Ali dared to be different. He caught the imagination of the world by refusing to do what was expected of him. And while at first people were shocked or appalled by him, eventually everyone grew to love him. Now he is remembered as a sports star who was the Greatest Of All Time.

THE G.O.A.T.

Oh I get it now!

If nobody dares to be different then nothing ever changes. People used to send messages attached to the feet of specially trained pigeons. We could have just carried on like that. But somebody invented the smartphone instead. Usually, people who invent new things get laughed at to start with. Why would anyone want a talking box in their house? Well, that's the TV. What do you think people thought when someone said: "Hey, I've got an idea for a global system of interconnected computer networks"? Sounds boring, but that's the Internet!

You probably remember the story by Hans Christian Andersen that shows what happens if we just go along with the crowd. Two weavers tell an emperor that they have made him some fabulous new clothes. The truth is they are very lazy and have not made anything at all, so they tell the emperor that only stupid people can't see the clothes they've made. Not wishing to appear stupid, the emperor says his new clothes are wonderful and pays the weavers.

The emperor then goes on parade in just his underwear. His subjects do not want to appear stupid either so they pretend they can see the clothes too.

Until one boy dares to be different.

He says the emperor has got nothing on! Realizing the boy is right the other people start to agree with him. The emperor is left red-faced because everyone has seen his pants.

The tale shows what can happen if you are so worried about fitting in that you just go along with everyone else.

In this chapter there are four stories about sports legends who dared to be different.

There is the motorcycle racer who won the world championship by doing something nobody had ever seen before. He wanted to

Then there is the brave Olympic diver who has been an inspiration to many by winning medals and standing up to bullies. He knows it is important to

BE A TREE.

We meet the jockey who made history in one of the toughest events of all because she understands that

SPORT IS FOR EVERYBODY.

And finally we hear the story of the world's greatest sprinter who was different in lots of ways. He became the coolest man in sport because he knew it was important to

THINK ABOUT YOUR DINNER!

LEGEND ID
MARC MÁRQUEZ

BORN: 17 February 1993

NATIONALITY: Spanish

SPORT: Motorcycle racing

LEGEND STATUS: Six-time MotoGP world

champion. Won the Moto2 and 125 cc world titles.

His brother Alex is also a top MotoGP rider.

MARC MÁRQUEZ DID not have time to blink at 200 mph. His eyes were wide open and staring at the back of the red bike of his great rival Andrea Dovizioso. He had to get past him. This was the 2018 Aragon Motorcycle Grand Prix in Spain, Marc's home race. His fans were standing up in the packed grandstands. They waved their flags decorated with his bike's number.

He knew the people in his home town of Cervera, near Barcelona, would be hanging number 93 banners from balconies and watching the race on big screens in the town square. He had to win, but Dovi, as he was known, was a tough opponent.

They went into a fast corner and Marc took his chance. He leant his bike over to the left so his knee and elbow were actually scraping the tarmac. The further he leant the faster he could go around the corner. But if he got it wrong and leant over by one centimetre too far then he would lose his balance and crash.

Marc always crashed a lot. He was known for it. He was brave and fearless, but he took big risks.

Dovi powered past him at another corner. Marc tried to sneak down the inside again when Dovi cut across him. Their bikes touched. Marc was forced to swerve. He had less than a second to save himself and so he ran off the track onto the slippery dirt. He felt the orange and white bike shaking under him but he kept his cool. He battled to regain his balance and edged back onto the track. Now the rider in third place had gone past him too. Marc's job had just got a lot tougher.

Marc believed in himself. He was only 25, but he had already won the world title four times. They called him "The Ant" because he was so small.

Ants can carry 50 times their own bodyweight.

A little help would be welcome by the way.

But Marc was strong too. Earlier that year, he had fallen while qualifying for the race. His bike had been destroyed in the crash. A member of his team arrived on a scooter and he hitched a ride back to the team garage.

He was back on his spare bike 137 seconds after the smash.

Then there was the race at Valencia where he had crashed and dislocated his shoulder. He was taken back to the pit area, where the teams worked on their bikes. He had the bone forced back into its socket. The pain was incredible. Normally doctors say anyone with a dislocated shoulder should avoid sport for at least six weeks.

Marc was back in six minutes.

Now in this race he was up to second place again and duelling with Dovi. He got into the lead but he had to brake too hard to make the corner. And then Dovi was in front again. With three laps left, Marc leant his bike over to the point where it was not safe any more.

The people watching in the grandstands, in the press box and back in Marc's town square all held their breath. But Marc did not crash. He went round that corner at unbelievable speed. He got into the lead and won the race by 0.6 seconds.

One race later, he would be the world champion again.

* * *

I WENT TO Spain to meet Marc in his sleepy home town a few months later. He met me in an office that doubled as his fan club base. He was wearing black jeans and a black denim jacket that highlighted his gleaming white smile. Down the road was the Marc Márquez Museum. He was a bit embarrassed about that!

I asked him how he had won so many races. He explained that he liked to

PUSH THE BOUNDARIES.

He meant that he went beyond what everyone else did or thought was possible. He was reaching new limits.

Marc rode his motorcycle in a special way. His secret was leaning his way around the corners. That kept his speed up whereas other riders had to slow down.

"Normally the angle is 59 degrees," he told me. "Over 60 and the tyres start to slide. Many times I am at 63 or 64. My team gets the data from the bike's computer. My data guy says: 'Be careful in this corner because you will crash'. I often save crashes when I am at 67 degrees. Every weekend I save a crash. But past 67 I have no chance."

Marc smiled a lot. Instead of fearing crashes, he had learnt how to fall. If he slid on his back he knew his leather suit would protect him. When he was hurt and had to ride with injuries, he said:

"You just find a way to adapt."

I discovered Marc was clever as well as brave. He said each race involved doing lots of quick sums. He liked maths at school and said he always tried to work out the answer in his head rather than using a calculator.

"On the circuit you need to be quick and smart. Technology can make us lazy."

For him being great at a sport was not all about being talented. Marc was a Barcelona football fan and his hero was Lionel Messi. He said: "Talent is only part of it. In training maybe there is someone with the same talent as [Messi]. But you have to use your talent under the biggest pressure. That is the hardest thing in sport."

Marc had found a way of riding that nobody else could match. He refused to accept that there was only one way to win a race. This is an amazing mindset to have in all areas of your life. Rather than giving up when you feel you aren't succeeding, try to think of a new way to complete the challenge. Find your angle. Dare to be different and hopefully it will be less painful than it has been for Marc! But pushing the boundaries has paid off for him.

In 2019, Marc won his sixth world title in a row.

★ LEGEND LESSON ★

PUSH THE BOUNDARIES.

Don't copy everyone else or do the same thing over and over again. Think of a new or different way to achieve your goal.

LEGEND ID

TOM DALEY

BORN: 21 May 1994

NATIONALITY: British

SPORT: Diving

LEGEND STATUS: World champion when he was only fifteen. Won the bronze medal in the 10 metre platform at the 2012 Olympics. Won bronze in the 10 metre synchro at the 2016 Olympics. Won four Commonwealth Games gold medals, three world titles and four European ones.

TOM DALEY WAS getting ready to jump off a ten metre outdoor diving platform. That's as high as your average two-storey house. It would be enough to frighten most people, but to make matters worse he was standing on his hands. Alongside him was his diving partner, Dan Goodfellow. This was the Commonwealth Games final in

Australia in 2018 and they had to get their timing perfect.

They needed to do four and a half somersaults before hitting the water together. This stuff took guts but Tom had been doing it for years. He was still only 23, but had been famous for most of his life.

He had been just fourteen when he went to the 2008 Olympic Games in Beijing, China.

His dad had bought him a ring to celebrate because he was too young to get an Olympic tattoo like lots of athletes did. He was still only eighteen when he won a bronze medal at the 2012 Olympics in London. And now he was after a fourth gold medal at the Commonwealth Games.

But Tom had a problem.

He had an injury. He had already had to pull out of one event because of it. And it was still very windy after a cyclone had hit the Gold Coast a few days earlier. Tom knew if he mistimed the jump then the impact could feel like landing on rock. He could cause terrible damage to his bad hip. He wanted the Commonwealth gold medal, but one wrong move and it would end in disaster. He counted down and then both he and Dan jumped.

The speed in each somersault was 60 mph.

Three metres from the water Tom and Dan released their legs.

They hit the water at 30 mph.

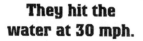

There was almost no splash.

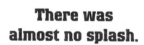

The pool was deep because they were jumping from such a great height. As I waited for them to surface, I thought about how much Tom had been through. Not only had he faced the physical pain of his injuries, but there were the mental obstacles created by bullies who had targeted him at school and more recently on social media. Tom needed to be resilient in every way.

When Tom surfaced he was smiling. His bad hip had survived the ten metre drop. The judges made some notes. The tension rose. Had they done enough? Then the marks flashed up. They had done it. Tom and Dan were the champions.

★ ★ ★

A FEW DAYS earlier I had gone to the Aquatics Centre to meet Tom. He was a fascinating person to talk to, but his cheery nature hid a lot.

As we chatted by the pool, Tom told me about his hip injury. He had got a dive wrong a few weeks beforehand and he had also banged his head on the water. The doctors had only just passed him fit to dive with Dan. He could not do the solo event because that involved a really complicated four-and-a-half-somersault dive. His damaged hip would not take that.

111

Tom told me how hard it was to stand at the top of a ten-metre board with doubts in your head.

"Do I get scared? Every single day. The day you are not scared is the day you hurt yourself."

Fear made him concentrate. Knowing what would happen if he let his mind wander kept him focused. His coach had some interesting advice for him. He said:

"BE A TREE."

His coach meant stand strong and still. And don't get blown over – by either the wind or the doubts in your head!

Tom had needed to be like a tree when he was growing up. He was different to the rest of the people at his school because he was a teenage star. He was often on TV and in the newspapers. Some people picked on him because of that. Bullies often target people who are different because, deep down, they are jealous or insecure.

They emptied Tom's pencil case and threw things at him when he stood up to speak in class. They called him "Diver Boy" and one boy even threatened to break his legs. "It's gone on a long time and reached a peak after the 2008 Olympics," he once said.

At the 2012 Olympics in London, Tom was eighteen and showed how brave he was again. He was preparing for his first dive in front of 18,000 people. He was a top medal chance. The TV and newspapers had been talking about this moment for years. As Tom counted down, the camera flashes all went off at the same time. He was distracted and fell awkwardly. The low score would have ruled him out of the competition, but his coach complained that he had been put off by the cameras. The judges said he could have another go. Imagine that pressure.

"My instant reaction was I didn't want to go back up there. I was the most terrified I have ever been in my life."

But by the time he reached the top of the platform, Tom was a tree again. He nailed that dive and got the bronze medal. It was a tremendous feat of courage.

Tom has also shown his courage in his personal life. He has spent most of his life bravely facing what others said about him. In 2013, he announced he was in a relationship with a man. He was famous by then and had his own YouTube channel that had 100 million views. In one interview he said:

"It's emotionally draining to have a secret."

When we met in Australia, Tom was married to Dustin Lance Black, and he was keen to speak up for the rights of LGBTQ+ people. The Commonwealth is a group of 54 countries, but in 37 of them it was still illegal to be gay. Tom thought people should be free to be their true selves.

He still got bullied. These days it was on social media. "I get tons of abuse every day but at the end of the day I'm married and I don't care what anyone says. I don't care if they don't like it."

Some sports stars have found it hard to come out as LGBTQ+. Many are afraid about receiving abuse in the stadiums or on social media.

Over the years, Tom has had to develop a thick skin to deal with negative comments. What helped him was having a support network. "I've always been surrounded by supportive people," he said.

His parents, his friends, his co-divers and now his husband had all helped him stand up to the bullies.

If you are struggling with bullies then remember that they pick on Olympic heroes too. And remember they are the ones with the problem. Get help from friends or family or teachers if you can. As Tom said, it can be draining to keep a secret to ourselves. It helps to share it with people who will support and help us. Even then it can be hard, but be brave, stand tall and be proud.

★ LEGEND LESSON ★

BE A TREE.

If you are being bullied try to stand up strong.
The support from others will help you achieve this.

LEGEND ID
BRYONY FROST

BORN: 13 April 1995

NATIONALITY: British

SPORT: Horse racing

LEGEND STATUS: The first woman to win a top Grade 1 race over jumps at the famous Cheltenham Festival. Won more than 100 races. In 2020, became the first woman to win the important King George VI Chase at Kempton.

BRYONY FROST WAS listening to her horse, Frodon, panting. Their breaths were in time. It was almost as if they were one. But now she could sense another horse catching them. This was the biggest race of Bryony's life and there were only a few jumps left. If she won she would be the first woman to win a top jumps race at the Cheltenham Festival, the biggest event of the year. It was 2019 and there were 60,000 people in the grandstands. She could hear them roaring as well as the thud of hooves on the turf.

Bryony liked surfing and rock climbing, but she loved horse racing most of all. And Frodon was her best friend. She knew that he was brave and fast, but they were up against the best.

It was like the Champions League of horses.

She glanced to her right as a horse called Aso caught them. Bryony gazed across and saw how determined he and his jockey looked. She felt her dream slipping away and her mind started to feel foggy. With two fences left, Aso had edged into the lead.

AND THEN SOMETHING AMAZING HAPPENED.

Frodon looked at Aso too. Eyeball to eyeball. And he pricked back his ears and picked up his legs. He accelerated. They came to the last fence. Frodon took off perfectly, brushed the top of it with his hooves and then landed well. Bryony hung on. She said:

"Come on mate!"

Suddenly, Aso appeared to be going backwards. His neck disappeared from Bryony's sight. Then his ears. Then his nostrils. And Frodon just got faster and faster.

Those seconds went by in a flash, but images from Bryony's life went through her mind. When she was nine, she had seen a clip of her dad riding a horse on YouTube. It was no ordinary race – it was the Grand National, the most famous horse race in the world, and her dad had won. She had grown up with horses. She would joke that her babysitter was actually a donkey called Nosey. And then there was the time a horse had nearly killed her when it had sat on her. She needed twelve operations after that, but she never gave up.

Now she could see the finishing post ahead. Frode, as she called him, was flying. She smiled and shouted:

"Now you're showing off!"

They crossed the line and Bryony patted his neck. Other jockeys slapped her on her back. The noise from the crowd was like thunder. I left the stand and rushed through the fans to the parade ring where the winning horses come afterwards. The crowd were chanting:

"FRODON! FRODON! FRODON!"

Your impressions of the race?

As Bryony and Frodon trotted past, I could see that she was crying with joy. She had mud all over her but she did not care. She had made history. Hers had been an astonishing story.

★ ★ ★

I WENT TO interview Bryony soon after her big win. I met her at the stables where Frodon lives in Devon. Bryony was good fun. She laughed a lot and spoke incredibly fast.

There are quite a few women jockeys, but people can be negative about them and think they aren't as good as the men. I asked Bryony if she cared what others thought. "Gender doesn't matter," she said. "I live by the metaphor about looking up the mountain. If you look up to the top then it is daunting. If I was a kid looking to this point where I am now I'd never have believed it."

She said you needed three things to climb the mountain.

"I don't see myself as different," she said. "I just see myself as me. I get annoyed with myself if I don't smile at someone because one smile makes two doesn't it? You have to keep improving and be a better person."

We were sipping coffee in a room decorated with paintings of famous horses. The real things trotted by outside the window. I knew she would rather be out there with Frodon, but she patiently told me her story.

Bryony was fifteen when another horse sat down on her and damaged her kidney. She recovered and went surfing, but felt terrible. Doctors found out she had a serious blood infection.

"My lungs felt like they were rotting."

It took her a long time to get better. And horse racing is one of the toughest sports. Jockeys can have 1,000 races a year and often ride with broken bones.

"My dad told me that if I was going to be a jump jockey then I had to learn how to fall so I would set up hay bales and deliberately throw myself off my pony."

Bryony actually had her arm in a sling when we met for the interview. Four days after winning on Frodon she fell off another horse and broke her collarbone.

It was just part of life for her, and a good lesson for us all. You will have ups and you will have downs. And if you are different, you might face more downs than others around you. But sometimes you just have to grin and bear it and take the falls.

Bryony dared to be different because she did not see any reason why only men could be the top jockeys. "I have not grown up to be a girl," she said. "I have two older brothers and my dad to keep up with. Poor Mum – she was so excited to get a girl and she turned out to be more like a bloke than her sons!"

Could she go on and become the champion jockey one day? Lots of people said a woman would never manage that because they did not have the physical strength. Bryony looked at her arm in the sling and said:

"I will take the falls, I already have."

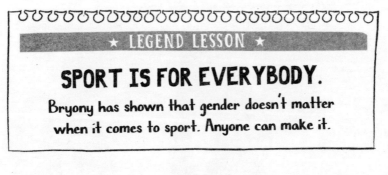

★ LEGEND LESSON ★

SPORT IS FOR EVERYBODY.

Bryony has shown that gender doesn't matter when it comes to sport. Anyone can make it.

LEGEND ID
USAIN BOLT

Born: 21 August 1986

Nationality: Jamaican

Sport: Athletics

LEGEND STATUS: The greatest sprinter of all time. Won eight Olympic gold medals in the 100 metres, 200 metres and 4 x 100 metres relay. Holds the world record for the 100 metres (9.58 seconds) and 200 metres (19.19 seconds). Also has eleven World Championship gold medals.

THE MOST THRILLING moment I have ever witnessed in sport was the one right before a 100 metres Olympic final. That's when the dreams of eight runners collide. A lifetime's work comes down to the next 10 seconds. For a moment, 80,000 people stop shouting and are quiet. That silence is golden.

In 2008, in the Bird's Nest Olympic stadium in Beijing, China, Usain Bolt was about to become a megastar. But eagle-eyed fans might have noticed something incredible.

One of his shoelaces was undone.

You would have expected him to make sure his shoes were tied before the Olympic final, but Usain *always* did things differently.

BANG!

The starter fired the fake gun to begin the race.
Thousands of flashes went off as people took photographs.
Usain expected his fellow Jamaican, Asafa Powell, to be close,
but he was nowhere. By halfway Usain had got past all his
rivals and he knew that he was going to win.

And then something inside his head clicked. Coaches
always tell sprinters to keep running as fast as they can all the
way to the line. They also tell them never to look sideways as
that can make them lose a fraction of a second.

But Usain shocked the world. He slowed down, put his
hands down by his side and then slapped his chest. Then he
looked sideways at his nearest rival!

Amazingly he still set a new world record:

9.69 seconds!

It only took him

41 steps.

His top speed was

28 mph.

Usain went to celebrate with the Jamaican fans. He was grinning as he pulled his Lightning Bolt pose, with one arm bent and another stretched out, to celebrate.

In the press box the journalists were all stunned too. And very quickly people began to ask just how fast he could have gone if he had not slowed down near the end.

That was the night that Usain Bolt became one of the biggest legends in sporting history. The following year he went even faster and set new world records for the 100 metres (9.58 seconds) and the 200 metres (19.19 seconds).

Those records still stood ten years later!

But back in Beijing not everyone was impressed. Jacques Rogge, the head of the International Olympic Committee, criticized Usain for showing off. He said: "That's not the way we perceive a champion to be."

Usain didn't care. When people asked how he coped with all the pressure at the start of the race he looked confused.

"It's not pressure. It's fun."

It was an important remark. I have interviewed lots of sprinters and they often seem under stress. They don't look like they enjoy what they do very much. Asafa Powell, for example, was a brilliant runner but he often messed up at the big championships. He let his nerves get to him. Usain said of his friend:

> **"He puts too much pressure on himself. Over the years he has been the top guy but he gets to the championships and he freaks out."**

From the moment Usain Bolt burst onto the world scene, he decided he was going to make sport more fun. That is what he was doing in China. He wasn't showing off. He was just being different.

He did not accept that athletes had to look oh-so serious. And he did not accept that he could never break the world record either.

Jacques Rogge may have said that Usain was cocky, but if he was not impressed with Usain, everybody else was. Other athletes started copying him and finding ways to celebrate. British runner Mo Farah did the Mobot where he made an "M" sign with his arms over his head. Yohan Blake, Usain's teammate, was nicknamed "The Beast". He started growling at cameras and pretending that he was a lion.

★ ★ ★

I HAVE MET Usain Bolt lots of times. The strangest time was in a bar in Germany where they had put sand on the floor to make it feel like Jamaica. Usain was always interesting. He told jokes. He was so laid back people found it hard to believe he was also the most explosive sports star in the world. He even told everyone that his secret was eating lots of chicken nuggets for dinner. He liked playing with people's expectations.

What I learnt from those interviews was that he didn't have an easy life before he was famous. As a boy, he had something called scoliosis. This meant that his spine formed an S shape instead of a straight line. It put extra pressure on his thighs and he kept getting injured. It also meant his right leg was over a centimetre shorter than his left one. That is not ideal for a runner because you need perfect balance. At least that is what people thought.

There was another problem too. Usain was 1.97 metres (6ft 5ins) tall. Most coaches felt the fastest runners were about 1.78 metres (5ft 10ins). When people saw his giant figure they did not think he would be very good at running. This is because you have to crouch down in the blocks at the start and then rise quickly to your full height. If you are tall and have long legs then this can be hard to do while keeping your balance. There was also an issue with his technique:

Usain Bolt was never a good starter.

I have seen him nearly fall over as he tried to get out of the blocks quickly with his long legs.

So let's look at the ways Usain Bolt was different to other runners:

He was too tall.

He slowed down in the most important race of his life.

He had fun.

He had problems with his back.

He forgot to tie his shoelace.

He had one leg longer than the other.

But the thing that made Usain really stand out as being different was the way he stayed so cool when everyone else was finding the situation stressful. He said that before a big race he just thought about lots of random things. One of them was what he was having for dinner that night. It helped him relax. Sometimes it relaxed him too much and that was why he forgot to do his shoelace before the Olympic final, but it was better than being so wound up and nervous that he could not perform. So let's add to that list of things that made him stand out.

He thought about chicken nuggets.

If we get too stressed it increases pressure and that affects our performance. So be different too. Make it fun. Take deep breaths, relax and be like Usain St Leo Bolt.

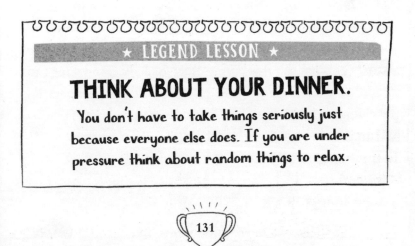

★ LEGEND LESSON ★

THINK ABOUT YOUR DINNER.
You don't have to take things seriously just because everyone else does. If you are under pressure think about random things to relax.

LEGEND HEADLINES:

FOOTBALL

Megan Rapinoe has won the World Cup twice with the USA as well as the Olympic gold medal in 2012. She could have been happy with that, but she has used her platform to speak out against injustices. In 2016, she knelt during the national anthem at a USA match to protest against racial inequality. She has also been a big supporter of LGBTQ+ causes. Megan has not been afraid to be a lone voice and has taken a stand for what she thinks is right – even if some people, including former President Trump, have criticized her for it.

HORSE RACING

Four months before the Magnolia Cup at Goodwood, **Khadijah Mellah** had never sat on a horse. On that day in 2019 she became the first British Muslim woman to ride in a major horse race. She was also the first jockey to ride wearing a hijab, the traditional head covering worn by some Muslim women. Khadijah won the race for amateur female jockeys on her horse, Haverland. She had broken down boundaries because she had been willing to take on new challenges. "I'd gone from zero to a hundred quickly," she said.

DARE TO BE DIFFERENT

MOTORSPORT

Niki Lauda won the Formula 1 world title in 1975. The following year he crashed in a race in Germany and the car burst into flames. He was pulled clear, put in a coma and almost died. He recovered but had terrible burns and had lost most of one ear. Some people made cruel comments and asked why he did not have cosmetic surgery to cover up the scars. Niki did not care. He said the scars were part of his life. It was what was inside that mattered. He only missed two races before he returned with his head covered in bandages. The following year Niki was the champion again.

TENNIS

Martina Navratilova played tennis differently to many women in the 1970s and 80s. She had a powerful game that involved a lot of running to the net and volleying. She realized this gave her an advantage against players who sat back on the baseline. Her tactics worked and she won eighteen Grand Slam singles titles. Martina was happy to stand out in different ways and has fought for equal rights for women. She also faced criticism for expressing her political views. She has always stood up for what she believed in.

CHAPTER 4:
GROWTH MINDSET

It's time to become a brain surgeon.

If we want to know how sports legends have got to the top we need to look inside their heads.

We have already met many different legends. They do lots of different sports and come from many different countries, but they all have one thing in common.

THEY HAVE A GROWTH MINDSET.

What this means is that they believe they can learn new things. They are open to ideas. They know that effort is important. *And they never give up.*

The opposite to this is a fixed mindset.

People with a fixed mindset don't think they can learn new things. They avoid challenges. They see training as a waste of time. They give up too easily.

Let me give you an example from working as a journalist. When a journalist goes to report on an evening football match, they have to write their report during the game. That's not easy. The next time you see a game on TV, try to write down what is happening while you are watching. Sometimes you miss things. On top of that, you have to tell the story well. As soon as the referee blows the final whistle, the journalist has to email their report to the newspaper office. Sometimes they will have to write 1,200 words during a 90-minute game.

That is 400 words every 30 minutes, or one word every 4.5 seconds!

When I started reporting, I found this really hard. I looked at the other writers who were finding it easy and despaired. I felt I didn't have time to think! But the more reports I wrote the more confident I became. In other words, I worked at it. In sport, people often argue about which is more important:

**TALENT
OR
TRAINING.**

It helps to have both. But you will become *better at anything* by working at it.

The brain is a living thing. It is also a supercomputer. It is more powerful than a MacBook or an Xbox. But it is also like a muscle in your arm or leg. It needs exercising. If you are a brilliant runner who sits on the sofa eating ice cream, your legs will not get stronger. And if you don't exercise your brain, then it will get soft and flabby too.

From meeting top sports stars I know how often they talk about their mindset. They know that unless they have a strong mind, their strong legs won't matter.

Let's use the legends we have already met to understand how a growth mindset works.

GROWTH MINDSET vs FIXED MINDSET

CHALLENGES

If you have a growth mindset you like challenges. They are opportunities to achieve new things. **ADAM PEATY** could have decided he would never beat the world record. Instead he created Project 56.

EFFORT

A growth mindset means you understand the need to try. A fixed mindset means you can't see the point. **JONNY WILKINSON** had natural ability but he still practised for hours and hours. He kicked thousands of penalties because he knew it would make him better.

FAILURES

If you have a fixed mindset you will think failures are the end of the world. You tell yourself you are a failure instead of realizing something has just not worked out. **KATARINA JOHNSON-THOMPSON** had "failed" before she became world champion. It did not stop her.

CRITICISM

Nobody likes to be criticized, but sometimes it can be useful. A fixed mindset either ignores criticism or thinks it defines them. A growth mindset learns from it. **ANTHONY JOSHUA** won back his boxing titles after learning from what he had done wrong in his first fight against Andy Ruiz.

Sometimes it is easy to believe you can't do something. You get labelled. The four sentences below are all evidence of a fixed mindset.

I can't do maths.

I can't kick with my left foot.

I can't play hockey.

I don't like speaking in class.

But add one word to the end of all those sentences and you can turn them into a growth mindset. And that word is:

YET.

In this chapter we will meet people whose growth mindset helped them achieve amazing things. There are the world-famous athletes born 55 years apart who turned the sporting world on its head with two mind-boggling records. They decided to

EMBRACE THE CHALLENGE.

There is the Paralympic star who refused to believe that disability could stop her from doing anything. She said:

"AIM HIGH EVEN WHEN YOU HIT A CABBAGE."

And we will be amazed by the story of the world's greatest footballer and the problems he faced, because

EVEN A GENIUS HAS TO WORK.

There is the rower who won three Olympic gold medals but now faced new challenges in a wheelchair. He decided to

MAKE A NEW NORMAL.

And we will see how a woman who dreamt of going to the Summer Olympics ended up travelling 80 mph down ice on something that resembled a tea tray instead. She explains:

"YOU CAN BE A SUMMER AND A WINTER PERSON."

LEGEND ID

ROGER BANNISTER

BORN: 23 March 1929 **DIED:** 3 March 2018

NATIONALITY: British **SPORT:** Athletics

LEGEND STATUS: First man to break the four-minute mile barrier. Gold medal at the 1954 British Empire Games. Famous doctor.

LEGEND ID

ELIUD KIPCHOGE

BORN: 5 November 1984

NATIONALITY: Kenyan **SPORT:** Athletics

LEGEND STATUS: First man to break the two-hour marathon barrier. Won the Olympic marathon in 2016. Four-time winner of the London Marathon.

ON 6 MAY 1954, Roger Bannister had a record-breaking plan. He was going to become the first man to run a mile in less than four minutes. For years runners had been trying to break that barrier. None had succeeded.

On the train ride from London to Oxford, Roger looked out of the window and noticed the trees bending in the wind. He decided that if the wind didn't drop, then he would postpone the record attempt. His coach, Franz Stampfl, was sitting in the carriage with him and ignored his concern about the wind. Franz knew other runners were trying to break the record too. John Landy was getting close in Australia. So was Wes Santee in the USA.

"You might not get another chance Roger," said Franz. "And if you pass it up today you may never forgive yourself for the rest of your life."

Half an hour before the race, it was still windy and Roger had not decided whether to run. Two friends were going to help him, but Chris Chataway and Chris Brasher were both growing frustrated with his dithering. "Come on Roger, make your mind up," they said.

Roger nodded. He'd do it. Before long they were all on the starting line. The world was watching. "Failure in sport can be almost as exciting to watch as success – provided the effort is absolutely genuine," Roger would later say.

Chris Brasher started at the front. The idea was for Roger to follow him. It is easier to run if you have someone in front dragging you along. Chris Brasher could run fast, but not for all four laps. He would drop back after two laps and then Chris Chataway would take over at the front for the third lap. Then Roger would have to run the last 300 yards on his own.

On the last lap, a strange thing happened to Roger. He said:

"My mind took over."

He felt that his mind raced ahead of his body and drew him forward. He no longer felt the pain in his legs.

Roger had just 59 seconds to complete that last lap and break the four-minute barrier. He said fear and pride drove him on. The clock was ticking. When he broke the tape, he collapsed into the arms of his friends. Now they just needed to wait for the time. When the announcer said:

"THREE MINUTES AND ..."

... the rest was lost in noise. He knew he had done it. The actual time was

The four-minute barrier had been broken!

Roger Bannister became one of the most famous people in Britain after that. His growth mindset had allowed him to believe he could do something that people thought was impossible.

And he was not finished when it came to developing his mindset, because after retiring from athletics he became a successful doctor.

★ ★ ★

I DROVE TO Oxford to see Roger in 2014. This was to mark the 60th anniversary of his famous run. Other athletes had since gone faster, but he had been the first. I sat in his lovely office and we had a cup of tea. He told me he was prouder about his work in medicine than his sporting achievements.

And then he told me something fascinating.

After the four-minute mile the next barrier that people thought could never be broken was the two-hour marathon. By the time we met in Oxford nobody had got close.

But Sir Roger, then 85 and a knight, told me somebody

would break the two-hour barrier within a few years. People thought he was mad for saying that, but he explained:

"It would be dead easy if they choose the perfect day on a straight track with the temperature about eighteen degrees."

He said that person would only need to beat the current world record by two per cent. It was possible.

I left Sir Roger thinking that he was a brilliant man. Most people would have been happy to be great at one thing. He had been great at running *and* medicine. He died in 2018. His prediction about breaking the two-hour marathon came true the following year.

★ ★ ★

LIKE SIR ROGER all those years before him, Eliud Kipchoge, a long-distance runner from Kenya, was bold enough to think outside the box.

Eliud accepted the challenge because he did not have a fixed mindset. And he did not give up when he faced obstacles. He persisted. He knew he was talented, but that would count for nothing if he didn't put in the effort. So he ran 160 miles a week to get ready to break the two-hour marathon.

"I think it is possible."

That's what Eliud said as he prepared to break the barrier on a perfect day in Austria, on the right track, with the right temperature. Just as Sir Roger had predicted. Eliud knew it was about keeping an open mind: "It is what is in your heart that matters."

On 12 October 2019, Eliud ran a marathon in

1 hour 59 minutes and 40 seconds.

He said: "After Roger Bannister made history, it took me another 65 years. This shows no one is limited."

People with fixed mindsets are not as limited as they think. You can be good at maths *and* literacy. You can be good at sport *and* then be a great scientist. People get labelled quickly, but you can do lots of things. And just because something is hard doesn't mean you can't do it.

We probably can't run like Roger and Eliud, but we can open our minds to our own challenges and break our own barriers.

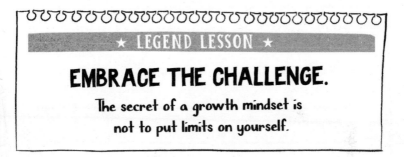

★ LEGEND LESSON ★

EMBRACE THE CHALLENGE.

The secret of a growth mindset is
not to put limits on yourself.

TANNI GREY-THOMPSON

BORN: 26 July 1969

NATIONALITY: British

SPORT: Wheelchair racing

LEGEND STATUS: Won eleven gold medals at the Paralympics. She also won the London Marathon six times.

IMAGINE WINNING THREE gold medals in five days. That is what Tanni Grey-Thompson did at the 2000 Paralympics in Sydney in Australia. This was the year when the Paralympics were becoming big news.

148

They were changing the way people saw disability.

When the Stoke Mandeville Games, which would develop into the Paralympics, began in 1948, disabled people were treated very differently by society. In many countries, those with disabilities were hidden away and not allowed to participate in everyday life. When she was growing up in the UK, Tanni had often been ignored because people thought there was something "wrong" with her because she was in a wheelchair. But now things were beginning to change.

Tanni had her three gold medals and was now on the starting line for the 400 metres. If she went home with four gold medals in a week the coverage of disabled sport would change for ever. There was a lot at stake for her and for millions of people.

Tanni has a condition called spina bifida. It caused her spine not to develop properly as a baby, leaving her with mobility problems. When she was young, she was able to walk, but that didn't stop people calling her "Limpy Legs". As she got older, her condition got more extreme. Her spine curved and it pulled on her ribs, changing the shape of her body.

149

Eventually, she needed to be in the wheelchair all the time. When she was thirteen, she needed an operation to put a metal rod into her spine. Afterwards she was put in a plaster cast that went from her hips up to her neck. She had to stay in that for six months, barely able to move. She said the worst thing about it was not being able to wash for that long.

When the doctors removed the plaster, she had lost lots of muscle. She turned to sport to grow stronger. She had tried lots of sports – tennis, swimming and horse riding – but when she first tried wheelchair racing she was hooked. She became obsessed and focused on athletics. She would get nervous for her entire career, but she loved racing.

In fact, Tanni always threw up before races. Her record was ten times!

She wasn't feeling good for the 400 metres in Sydney. She went to the side of the track and vomited. She felt jittery too. Her nerves weren't helped by the fact she had been drawn in lane eight. It is usually harder to win from the outside lane because you can't see what the other athletes are doing.

She said to her friend, Doc Campbell, that she didn't even want to be there. "Typical athlete," he said.

Then they were away. Tanni started hard. She had racing gloves on and she turned her wheels as quickly as she could. She kept her head down and just raced like she had done a thousand times before.

When she came out of the bend she looked up and used the big screen in the stadium to see where the others were. One of her rivals, Madeleine Nordlund, was still with her. She put her head back down and pushed with all her might.

As she came off the last bend she glanced at the big screen at the other end of the stadium. She felt a burst of excitement when she saw Madeleine had started to fade away. Tanni was clear. She kept pushing and crossed the line. She had done it.

FOUR GOLD MEDALS IN EIGHT DAYS!

★ ★ ★

I GOT TO KNOW Tanni after that and helped her write a book about her life. She came to talk to me at my house and my little daughter, Erin, would climb over her wheelchair. She was very cool. She wore purple Doc Martens boots and dyed her hair different colours. She did not like to think that she was extraordinary. She was just a sportsperson like all the others.

She had never thought "Why me?" about her disability. I asked Tanni about having spina bifida, and she said her attitude was:

"I've got it and there's nothing I can do about it so I might as well get on with it."

Being in a wheelchair had never stopped her doing anything she wanted to.

Tanni had a growth mindset. She was always willing to take on new challenges and never let obstacles get in her way. And her success at the Paralympics in 2000 was a major stepping stone towards people understanding more about disability.

She told me that sometimes people assumed she was stupid or incapable just because she was in a wheelchair. One person patted her on the head. Another called her "my little friend". One day she was waiting at the counter in a clothes shop and an assistant ignored her. When Tanni asked why, the woman said that she was waiting for Tanni's carer. Tanni didn't need a carer – she was completely independent. Her car was parked outside.

Tanni knew it was important to have disabled people in the public eye so we all understood they were just like everyone else. She said that many years ago disabled children were abandoned. Some were even left to die. Now that had changed, but she believed that:

"People are frightened by disability."

Because people did not know much about disability, they saw it as something strange or scary. But it's neither of those things.

After 2000, the links between the Olympics and Paralympics started to grow. Tanni's success helped people change how they thought about disability.

Now people realize that Paralympic athletes shouldn't be defined be their disability – they are elite athletes, just like all the others. And wheelchair racing is one of the most exciting sports you will ever see with high speed action, lots of crashes and nail biting finishes.

Tanni told me something brilliant, that I've never forgotten. Her grandfather was called Dubby Jones and he would say:

"Aim high even if you hit a cabbage!"

It was an odd saying. What he meant was you should set your sights high even if you end up on the ground where the cabbages grow. Tanni said she always did this.

Four years later, in the 2004 Athens Olympics in Greece, she won two more gold medals to become Team GB's most successful track Paralympic athlete. But her growth mindset made her seek out new challenges. She went on to sit in the House of Lords where she helped form new laws to help disabled people. She continues to grow by setting new goals and she always aims high.

★ LEGEND LESSON ★

AIM HIGH EVEN IF YOU HIT A CABBAGE.

A growth mindset means you can learn to do any new skill. So set your goals high. If you fall short you will still have gone a long way.

LEGEND ID
LIONEL MESSI

BORN: 24 June 1987

NATIONALITY: Argentinian

SPORT: Football

LEGEND STATUS: One of the greatest footballers of all time. Won six Ballon d'Or awards and more than 30 trophies for Barcelona. Scored more than 600 goals for club and country.

IT WAS THE Champions League final of 2011. Lionel Messi and his Barcelona team were playing Manchester United at Wembley Stadium. Both teams had already won their league titles. It was a clash of the giants, but the most important person was the smallest player on the pitch.

Lionel had already established himself as the greatest player in the world. By the time of that match in 2011, he had won two Champions League finals, five Spanish league titles and two Ballon d'Or trophies, which are awarded to the best player in the world that year.

But beating Manchester United would be tough. They had good players like Wayne Rooney and Rio Ferdinand. Barca, as the Spanish called their team, would need to play well. And they needed Leo, as his friends called him, to be on top form.

As everyone expected, Barca had more of the ball. They passed it around and Manchester's players chased after them. Everybody was giving everything they had. This was the biggest prize in club football.

Glory was only 90 minutes away...

Barca took the lead when Pedro fired a low shot past Edwin van der Sar in the Manchester goal. The Spanish fans waved their giant purple and yellow flags and made a huge noise. Then the ball fell to Rooney inside the Barca area and he struck a first-time shot into the top corner.

1–1

It stayed like that until half-time, until Leo changed everything. He may have been small, but he had perfect control and he was fast. He tormented the Manchester defence. After 54 minutes his friend Andres Iniesta rolled a short pass to him. Leo was around 35 yards from the goal and there were ten Manchester players in front of him. He knew what to do. He moved to his left at speed and then, as Patrice Evra came to tackle him, he fired in a low shot with his left boot. It curled away from the tall goalkeeper and into the corner. He had hit it just hard enough and at the perfect angle. He ran off to the crowd to celebrate.

After that the game became

THE MESSI SHOW!

Nobody could get close to him. He danced down the right wing and created a third goal. Barca won 3–1 and Leo was the champion of Europe again.

★ ★ ★

I WATCHED HIM play and wondered how he did it. Football was getting more physical and the players were bigger and more muscular. But Leo, despite being short and slight, was still the best.

In 2013, I was in Argentina and decided to go to Leo's home city of Rosario to find some answers. His old house was in a run-down area. Stray dogs sniffed along the streets. Graffiti about Rosario's two big football teams – Central and Newell's Old Boys – covered the walls. I even saw the hole in the fence that Leo and his friend Cintia would climb through on their way to school.

I knocked on a door and met Cintia's grandfather. He was called Ruben Manicabale and he said Leo was always playing barefoot football in the street. "Once he came back here and there was no ball so he pulled a lemon from a tree and started juggling." On another occasion it was said Leo did 113 keepy-uppies with an orange.

But there was a serious problem when Leo was a boy. He stopped growing. He was so small compared to other boys his age that he got a new nickname: "Flea".

I take this as a compliment!

His club, Newell's Old Boys, got in touch with a doctor called Diego Schwarzstein. I decided to ask him what had happened next.

Dr Schwarzstein had a fancy office with expensive paintings on the walls. We sat down and he told me that Leo had a hormone deficiency. Hormones are chemicals that regulate our bodies and Leo would need daily injections to help him grow. The injections cost $1,000 (US) for a 45-day programme. That was too much for Leo's father, Jorge, who was a steelworker.

At first Newell's helped and Leo would take a blue cooler containing his medicine to every match. Dr Schwarzstein was a football fan and his favourite player was Diego Maradona, who was also small. Leo asked him: "Will I be tall enough?"

The doctor replied: "You will be taller than Maradona – but I don't know if you will be better."

Newell's did not have enough money to help Leo for long, but mighty Barcelona could. So at the age of just thirteen, Leo went for a trial thousands of miles away from home on a different continent.

Think about how hard this must have been. His beloved grandmother, Celia, had recently died. He was at a physical disadvantage to the other players, in a foreign country and had to have injections to help him grow. In his trial he would face some of the best young players in the world.

He needed a growth mindset in every way.

He needed to believe he could grow mentally and physically. Even though he was full of nerves and he was homesick, he still looked at the obstacles as challenges.

Some of the other players at the trial laughed at him. Cesc Fabregas was there. He would become a great player for Barcelona, Arsenal and Chelsea. He called Leo "The Mute", because he was too shy to speak. Even the coaches watching from the sidelines said: "He's too small." But then he started to play. Fabregas could get nowhere near him. The coaches were amazed. They said:

"This boy could be a sensation!"

It was decided that Leo would sign a junior contract and he would move to Spain. At first his parents and brothers and sisters went with him, but before long it was just him and his dad.

In that office in Rosario, his old doctor told me: "The medicine was not a problem for him. It was just like a diabetic giving himself daily doses of insulin." He said:

"The mental pain of leaving was far worse. That was emotionally very hard."

Leo did not let the hurdles or name-calling get in the way of his growth mindset. He wanted to be a footballer and he put all his efforts into achieving that. Three years later, at only sixteen he played for Barcelona's first team in front of 90,000 people at the huge Camp Nou stadium.

He would go on to score more than 600 goals for Barcelona and Argentina. He won the Ballon d'Or six times. He would win the Champions League Final in 2011 and then again in 2015, as well as many other league titles.

He was still small – only 5ft 7ins – but he never stopped working. He knew he could be better. He still wants to win the World Cup with Argentina. He said:

"The day you think there are no improvements to be made is a sad one for any player."

Leo could have given up. He could have stayed in Argentina because he was scared to leave home. He could have listened to all the people saying he was too small. If anyone ever tells you that you do not fit in then remember that the world's greatest footballer was told the same. And if you are good at something do not sit back and relax. The best work even harder because they know talent is not something that is static. It can change and grow. It does not matter if you are too small or too big for something as long as your attitude is right. There is an old saying in sport:

It is not the size of the dog in the fight that counts – it is the size of the fight in the dog.

★ LEGEND LESSON ★

EVEN A GENIUS HAS TO WORK.
Talent is not enough. Everyone faces problems, but the best see them as opportunities.

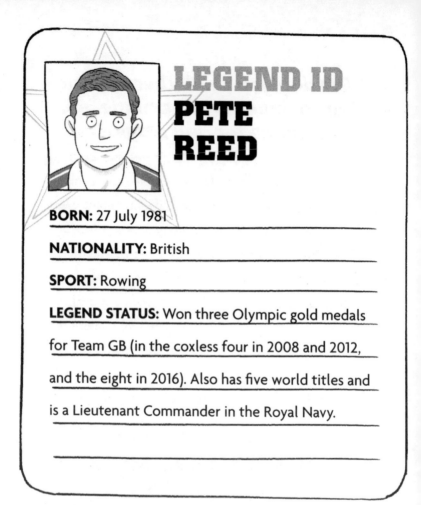

LEGEND ID

PETE REED

BORN: 27 July 1981

NATIONALITY: British

SPORT: Rowing

LEGEND STATUS: Won three Olympic gold medals for Team GB (in the coxless four in 2008 and 2012, and the eight in 2016). Also has five world titles and is a Lieutenant Commander in the Royal Navy.

DOWN AT THE Lagoa Rodrigo rowing lake the rain had stopped and the sun had come out. It was a beautiful day at the 2016 Olympics in Rio de Janeiro, Brazil and Pete Reed was ready. He was in the number 4 seat in the Team GB's men's eight boat. There were two kilometres of lung-sapping action between him and a third Olympic gold medal.

Two seats behind him was Andrew Triggs Hodge. He was Pete's great friend and they had been in the coxless fours that won gold medals in 2008 and 2012. I had interviewed them both before the 2008 Olympics when they did some fitness tests at the Navy Training Centre. Pete had blown into a machine called a vitalograph. It measured his lung capacity. The needle went off the scale.

"That's not happened in 20 years!" the shocked doctor said.

Pete even made the *Guinness World Records* for having a lung capacity of 11.68 litres. That was about double the average person and showed just how fit he was. He had a lot of puff!

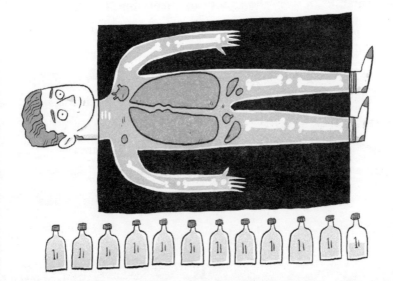

Eight years on and Pete was blowing hard again as he helped his team down the lake in the final in Rio. The German team were the European champions. The Dutch boat was also very strong. But the eight British men were rowing perfectly. They picked up the pace, all their oars in time, and edged ahead.

They crossed the line and started high-fiving and slapping each other on the back. For Pete and Andrew this was their third gold medal in a row. It was a remarkable achievement spanning eight years of hard work.

I thought about all their training. I also thought back to that day in 2008 at the training centre when Pete told me how hard he worked on a rowing machine.

"I've felt pain all through my body and passed out on the floor. You lie there not able to move, trying to breathe, trying to move your feet, but they hurt so much."

I thought about those words again when disaster struck for Pete in 2019.

Pete retired from rowing in 2018 and was continuing his career in the Navy. He was a Lieutenant Commander and was getting ready to do a commando obstacle course. Suddenly, he felt like he had a belt strapped tightly across his chest. He was rushed to hospital where he suffered two strokes. A stroke is when the blood supply to the brain gets cut off and it can have many serious, long-lasting effects.

The second stroke left Pete paralysed and in a wheelchair. From being not far off Superman, he was told he would never walk again.

★ ★ ★

TWO MONTHS AFTER the stroke I went to interview Pete. I wanted to know how he was coping. In the hospital in Salisbury, he wheeled towards me. We shook hands. "I'm sorry I can't get up," he joked.

Most people in his situation might have felt sorry for themselves. Pete had been one of the fittest men on the planet. He was a triple Olympic champion and a top Navy officer. Now he said the doctors had told him he would need to use a wheelchair for the rest of his life. But Pete was not the sort to give up without a fight.

> *I'm not going to say I'm going to be running marathons or clambering up mountains but can I walk again? I don't know – but I back myself.*

Pete said that he was treating his recovery as if he was training for the Olympics. He had to put the work in. And he had to look for tiny improvements each day, not giant steps. One of the effects of his stroke was it was hard to control his bowels. He was keeping a diary. "One of my entries from week one is, 'I didn't poo the bed today'. They are positive things that can't be seen but they are massive wins."

It was inspiring talking to Pete. He did not feel sorry for himself because he could not use his legs. He was just glad he could still use his arms. Part of having a growth mindset is being able to look at things in different ways.

★ ★ ★

FOUR MONTHS LATER I interviewed Pete again. He said he and his girlfriend Jeannie were happier than they had ever been. He was still using his wheelchair but he was embracing the challenge. "In my right foot I can move all my toes," he said.

He said he was still a long way off walking, but managed to stay positive by not looking back. He knew that he could create his own mood by how he thought about things. Pete said: "The thing is not to dwell on how things were or what you haven't got."

This is a strategy we can use in our lives, even if our challenges are not as serious as Pete's. Two people can look at the same thing and see it very differently. It depends on your mindset. Pete said whenever he started to feel that life wasn't fair he would stop himself. "I may never fully accept what has happened, but I can keep my mind under control when its runs away from me."

His trick was to find something positive to think about. It might be a tiny thing. He had taken up baking and photography so for him it might be a tasty cake or a nice picture. Or it might be feeling his toes again.

"You can change direction and it's easy to go downhill. But the smallest bit of uphill matters and very quickly you start getting towards the top of your mountain."

Pete's life had been changed in the most dramatic way. If he had a fixed mindset he would have been bitter about his experience and felt terrible about being in a wheelchair. Instead, he saw what had happened as a new challenge. With every setback he persisted. He said: "I'm making a new normal."

We can all find a new normal. We think we are on one path, but we can just as easily find happiness and success if we go down another one. We just need to be open to new adventures.

★ LEGEND LESSON ★

MAKE A NEW NORMAL.

You can adapt to any situation by resetting your goals.

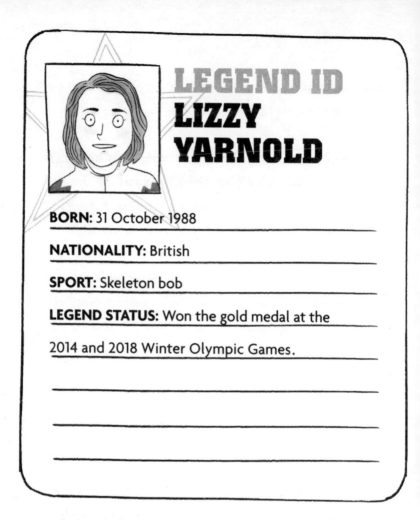

LEGEND ID

LIZZY YARNOLD

BORN: 31 October 1988

NATIONALITY: British

SPORT: Skeleton bob

LEGEND STATUS: Won the gold medal at the
2014 and 2018 Winter Olympic Games.

IT WAS FRIDAY night under the floodlights at the Sochi
Sliding Centre in Russia at the 2014 Winter Olympics and
Lizzy Yarnold was half a minute away from winning the
most important race of her life.

She wasn't frightened – but I would have been terrified.

Lizzy's skeleton race involved plunging head first down a hard ice track clinging to the top of tiny sled called a bob.

It was like racing down ice on a tea tray at 80 mph.

The strange thing was that Lizzy had dreamt of going to the Summer Olympics NOT the Winter Olympics. She wanted to be a heptathlete like Katarina Johnson-Thompson, but she had not been quite good enough. In 2012, when Jessica Ennis-Hill won the Olympic heptathlon gold medal, Lizzy had been the 54th best shot-putter in Britain.

She had a growth mindset, though, and had found her talent. Her friends thought she was mad because her new sport was so dangerous.

In the skeleton the G-force was the same as in a jet fighter!

Her great rival Noelle Pikus-Pace had already been injured in Sochi. The American had hit her head on the ice wall while flying down the track. She needed a brain scan before being passed fit to carry on. Lizzy, too, had suffered lots of injuries and had a serious back problem that had once left her unable to move for hours.

But this was her time. The crowd rang their cow bells. Lizzy's mum and dad, Judith and Clive, crossed their fingers. The journalists in the freezing press centre in Sochi watched the monitors. At home in England, her two nans watched the TV. The anticipation rose. Her lead was 0.78 seconds after the first three runs.

There was one descent left. She had to get it right.

She flew down the track, her body perfectly centred on the bob. It was smooth and she kept her line. The seconds ticked by. The adrenaline kicked in.

By the side of
the track, a woman named
Amy Williams watched. Four
years earlier, at the 2010 Winter
Olympics in Vancouver, Canada, Amy
had won the gold medal on her sled
which she called Arthur. She once told me
she would obsess about Arthur and even argue
with him. She said her boyfriend didn't mind!
Now Amy owned the flat where Lizzy lived.
She was helping her repeat her success.

Lizzy crossed the line.

Her total lead was 0.97 seconds.

She had demolished the opposition.

LIZZY WAS A bundle of excitement afterwards. It was an incredible tale. How had Great Britain, a country with no ice tracks and no real history in winter sports, become the best in the world at skeleton?

It is one of the greatest stories about a growth mindset and it began years earlier in 2002.

ALEX COOMBER had been in the Royal Air Force and wanted to try her hand at a sport called luge. This is like very fast sledging. The difference with skeleton is that in the luge you go down feet first. But there were no places left at a luge open day and so she tried skeleton instead. She ended up making her own bob from a tea tray and the handles from a disabled toilet. At the 2002 Winter Olympics at Salt Lake, USA, she won a bronze medal.

SHELLEY RUDMAN watched that and decided she wanted to have a go too. Luckily, the people in her village helped her by holding events to raise the money she needed. She went to the 2006 Winter Olympics in Turin, Italy. She won a silver medal in the skeleton.

Then came **AMY WILLIAMS**. A science student called James Roche designed a sled for her. This was Arthur and Amy won gold in Canada in 2010. Lizzy was away competing that night and stayed up until 3 a.m. to watch the race on TV.

These three women refused to accept that having no money or snow were obstacles that could not be overcome.

But Lizzy had gone even further. She had to change her dream when she accepted she was on the wrong path. She did it because UK Sport, the people who run Olympic sport, decided they wanted to find new champions.

They wondered if some of the best people were actually doing the wrong sport.

They set up a scheme called

Girls4Gold.

This was to encourage top athletes to try new sports. Lizzy was a heptathlete when she filled out a questionnaire. She had to do a 30-metre sprint. When she was told she had made the final round of selection for the skeleton, she didn't even know what the event was!

Why are they giving me a tea tray?

It didn't matter. She had the basic things that you needed. She was fast and brave.

She was also willing to learn.

By the time she won gold she had done around 1,500 descents. She had relished the obstacles.

Yet Lizzy did not stop there. She won the Winter Olympics gold medal again four years later in 2018 in PyeongChang in South Korea. But it was not easy. Her back pain had got worse and she needed an operation.

"It wasn't just the physical pain — but realizing that I'm not able to tie my shoelaces."

She felt helpless. It was only opening up to her mum and telling her how bad she felt that made it easier.

"We enjoy amazing highs, but athletes are human and can be vulnerable too."

She used her growth mindset again, just as she had when starting the skeleton. She took on the new challenges. It is an important message. Even the strongest and bravest people sometimes feel weak and scared. But just tell yourself that you can grow from the difficult experiences.

Lizzy has never stopped taking on challenges.

She was fascinated by numbers and said she now wanted to get a job as a tax inspector!

★ LEGEND LESSON ★

YOU CAN BE A SUMMER AND A WINTER PERSON.

You don't have to restrict yourself to one thing.

LEGEND HEADLINES:

BASKETBALL

Kareem Abdul-Jabbar is the highest point-scorer in the history of the NBA, basketball's greatest league. He scored 38,387 points, but he once told me: "If basketball was all I could do with my life I'd be very limited." His list of other achievements is long – he beat cancer, he became a father, he starred in the hit film *Airplane!*, he wrote a novel about the famous detective Sherlock Holmes and is a leading figure calling for equal rights for Black people in the USA. He never restricted himself to one thing.

SWIMMING/ CYCLING

Sarah Storey was born without a fully-functioning left hand. She became a star when she won two gold medals at swimming at the 1992 Paralympics in Barcelona, Spain. She kept winning, but then developed an ear infection that meant she could no longer swim. Instead of giving up, she reset her goals and found a new sport: cycling. By the time she retired she had won five Paralympic gold medals for swimming and nine for cycling, passing Tanni Grey-Thompson's record Paralympic haul for a British woman. She realized she could be just as good – if not better – at a new sport.

GROWTH MINDSET

SAILING

Ellen MacArthur was not brought up near the sea but fell in love with sailing after reading a book about boats called *Swallows and Amazons*. In 2005, when she was only 28, she set a world record for sailing around the world on her own. It took her 71 days 18 minutes and 33 seconds. On her boat she could only sleep for 20 minutes at a time because she had to keep lookout! Ellen kept pushing herself. She set up a trust to help people who were recovering from cancer regain their confidence through sailing. Then she set up a foundation to help the world by fighting plastic waste and pollution.

SWIMMING

Natalie du Toit had to have her left leg amputated when she was seventeen after a car accident. She was already a talented swimmer and three years later won five gold medals at the 2004 Paralympics. Natalie had other ambitions, though. She wanted to compete at the Olympic Games and show that disability was not a barrier to anything. In 2008, she got her wish when she swam in the 10 kilometre open water race at the Olympic Games in Beijing, China. She retired with thirteen Paralympic and twelve World Championship gold medals.

CHAPTER 5:
THE CONFIDENCE TRICK

How do sports legends succeed?

They imagine they have a monkey in their head.

Confidence is the belief that you can do something. It's a great thing, but it is not easy to get and it's even harder to keep. Even the people you think are really confident sometimes struggle. The trouble is we all have what a leading sports scientist, Dr Steve Peters, calls

THE INNER CHIMP.

Your brain is divided into two sections. There is the human part, which is the thinking bit. This is the bit you use when you are reading something or trying to do a puzzle. Scientists call it the logical section.

Then there is the part that is all about emotions. This is how you feel. It is about acting impulsively without thinking things through. It is the bit of your brain that tells you lots of negative things. And this is the part of the brain that Dr Peters calls the monkey section. It's the bit that causes trouble.

I have met lots of sports stars who say they work hard to keep their inner chimp under control. They know that if they listen to the chimp it can ruin their chances.

Take the case of Chris Hoy.

In 2004, Chris Hoy, the brilliant British cyclist, was struggling with his confidence. He went to see Dr Peters and had a brain scan. It showed that when he was emotional the blood flowed to the right side of his brain. When he was relaxed and trying to think carefully about something it went to the left. The left is the side of the brain responsible for logic. Chris knew from the scan that if he got emotional he could lose concentration. He needed the left bit of his brain to work best when he was riding. He told Dr Peters:

"When I let my enormous inner chimp out before races I started thinking irrationally with a tremendous sense of foreboding – wondering about all the 'what ifs', crashes and mistakes."

How did he control his chimp so he could think positively? He used a technique called

VISUALIZATION.

Instead of letting his inner chimp run wild and think

about all the things that could go wrong, he imagined (or *visualized*) the perfect race.

It worked. Chis Hoy won six Olympic gold medals.

The more sportspeople I have met, the more I realize how many suffer from a lack of confidence. Remember Katarina Johnson-Thompson thinking she did not belong at the top? Or how Jonny Wilkinson was worried that he would let everyone down?

Jonny also visualized things. I know this from interviewing Jonny's kicking coach, Dave Aldred. He told Jonny to imagine a line from the ball to the middle of the posts. He also said the problem with a lot of rugby coaches was that they told players what they *didn't* want them to do.

"They say 'don't drop the ball' but they should be telling them what they want them to do. The power of language is important. It's dynamite in the right hands."

Telling yourself not to do something is unhelpful. Try not thinking about a pink elephant. What's the first thing you think about? A pink elephant. You need to tell yourself how you are going to achieve something, not what might go wrong.

There are lots of tricks to improve your confidence. Using positive language is part of it. So is visualizing the result you want. Then you might try something called anchoring. This is when you do the same thing before a task. I knew one runner who always scratched his ear before a race to tell himself he was ready and it was time to concentrate. Adam Peaty told himself to burn the boats.

BUT THE MOST IMPORTANT THING OF ALL IS TO TAME THE INNER CHIMP.

This is the big one if you want to be confident. You need to stop your doubts and the negative stuff you say to yourself.

In this chapter we will discover the football team who were seen as no-hopers, but had the confidence to take on the billionaire giants of English football. They learnt to

NEVER SAY CAN'T.

There is the rugby player who was born with a disability and was always in trouble at school. She worked at her confidence by repeating key phrases. She

GOT A MANTRA.

We will hear about one of greatest tennis players of all. She developed confidence about her body image by realizing she had to

TAKE CONTROL.

And finally there is the hockey star who became the penalty shoot-out queen because of a little black book. She knows you have to

DO YOUR HOMEWORK.

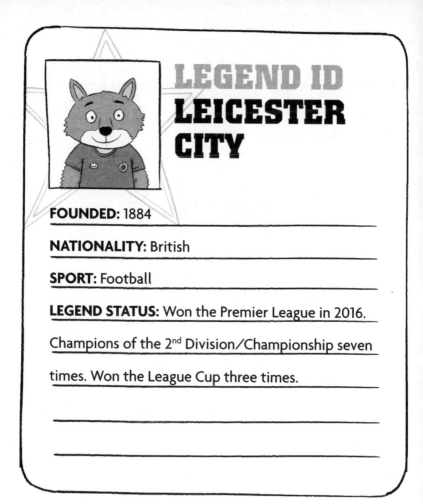

LEGEND ID
LEICESTER CITY

FOUNDED: 1884

NATIONALITY: British

SPORT: Football

LEGEND STATUS: Won the Premier League in 2016. Champions of the 2nd Division/Championship seven times. Won the League Cup three times.

NOBODY THOUGHT Claudio Ranieri was the right man for the job when he was revealed as Leicester City's new manager in 2015. His last job had been with the Greece national team, but he had been sacked when they lost to the Faroe Islands, a tiny country with a population of only

50,000 people. Claudio's last job in the Premier League had been thirteen years before at Chelsea. The man who took over from him as manager, José Mourinho, went as far as to call him a

LOSER!

Even old Leicester stars were not impressed. Gary Lineker had been the star striker for the team. He tweeted:

"Claudio Ranieri? Really?"

Lots of sports journalists said they thought Leicester would get relegated with Claudio in charge. The odds of them winning the Premier League were

5,000–1.

That meant that if Leicester played the league once a year for 5,000 years they would probably win it once. They were no-hopers. One reporter said:

"How Claudio Ranieri continues to land good jobs is a mystery."

Leicester's team had not cost much money and there weren't many great players. They could not stop the other team scoring in their first nine games.

Then Claudio had an idea. He said he would buy every player a pizza if the team kept a clean sheet.

Leicester beat Crystal Palace 1–0. Jamie Vardy scored the goal that won the match. Afterwards Claudio took the team to Peter Pizzeria in Leicester.

I had a surprise for them when we got there. I said, 'You have to work for everything. You work for your pizza, too. We will make our own'. So we went into the kitchen with the dough and the cheese and the sauce. We tossed our own pies. I love my pizza and my pasta. Now, we make a lot of clean sheets.

Claudio wanted his team to realize they had to work for everything. He also wanted them to have fun. His strategy worked and they kept winning matches. That didn't stop people being negative about their chances.

Robbie Savage, another former Leicester player, had a radio show. He said it was impossible for Leicester to win the league.

"It can't happen."

But he was wrong. It was not impossible. It was just improbable, which means not likely. They are different things. Leicester's players never said can't. Remember what Dave Aldred, the rugby coach, said. Words can be dynamite if used properly.

Apart from one year when Blackburn Rovers had been champions, the only teams who had won the Premier League were Manchester United, Arsenal, Chelsea and Manchester City. They spent millions of pounds on the world's best players.

After the Crystal Palace game, Leicester lost only once in their next fifteen matches. Claudio kept things simple. He knew he did not have the best players, but he could still have the best team. He encouraged the players to be friends so they would try harder for each other. He went to their birthday parties. He made it seem like a family.

And Jamie Vardy kept scoring. Riyad Mahrez was also playing brilliantly. He had admitted he did not know anything about Leicester before he joined the club.

He said the city was more famous for its rugby club!

192

Even when Leicester reached the top of the Premier League, people still didn't think they would last.

In December 2015, Gary Lineker said that if Leicester won the league he would present the football programme "Match of the Day"…

IN HIS UNDERPANTS!

By May 2016, Leicester had an eight-point lead over second-place Tottenham Hotspur. So on a Monday night the players all gathered at Jamie Vardy's house to watch Tottenham play Chelsea on TV. If Tottenham lost or drew, then Leicester would be champions for the first time.

Tottenham started well. They went 2–0 up. But Chelsea's Gary Cahill scored after 58 minutes. With seven minutes left, Eden Hazard then scored Chelsea's second goal. The match was a draw. Leicester had won.

THE PARTY STARTED.

I USED TO live in Leicester. Friends who were fans were stunned. I remembered how we had watched Leicester play in the lower leagues in run-down grounds when they had little hope. Now there were street parties and parades.

All journalists liked going to Leicester and were excited about the unexpected shake-up of the League. Every club provides free food for the media. At Leicester, this included delicious cakes and pies. We all agreed they were also the title winners when it came to doing lunch!

I was most pleased for Claudio Ranieri. He was always polite and funny in interviews and he had faced all the negative things people had said about him and come out triumphant.

Robbie Savage admitted he had got it wrong.

José Mourinho, the man who had called Claudio a loser, was sacked by Chelsea – after his team lost to Leicester.

How had Claudio pulled off this miracle? In our press conference, he explained that part of it was down to boosting confidence by setting small goals.

To start with Leicester aimed for 40 points because that would be enough to mean they would not get relegated. When they got 40, and they felt more confident, Ranieri began to target the top seven which would mean they qualified for a place in Europe the next season. Only when they had achieved that did they start to think about winning the league.

Watch your words next time, Gary!

He also made sure his players trained hard and remembered to concentrate. That was why his catchphrase became:

DILLY-DING, DILLY-DONG!

Claudio said this at training if players were not working hard enough. It was meant to sound like a bell. It meant

WAKE UP!

He even gave the players a bell for Christmas. Each one was engraved with their name. It was a reminder to keep working hard and stay focused on their jobs.

There are lots of lessons we can learn from Leicester. These include:

★ **NEVER GIVE UP.** The club motto is "foxes never quit".

★ **SET SMALL GOALS** to gain confidence before focusing on the biggest one.

★ **ENJOY** the work. You are much more likely to do something well if you are having fun.

★ **IGNORE** what everyone else is saying and doing. This is the most important of all. Leicester's players did not compare themselves to the other stars who cost more money in transfer fees. They did not believe Robbie Savage when he said they couldn't win. Anything is possible and confidence can make you feel like a world-beater.

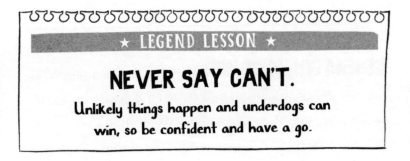

★ LEGEND LESSON ★

NEVER SAY CAN'T.
Unlikely things happen and underdogs can win, so be confident and have a go.

LEGEND ID
SERENA WILLIAMS

BORN: 26 September 1981

NATIONALITY: American

SPORT: Tennis

LEGEND STATUS: Won 23 Grand Slam singles titles (Wimbledon seven times, Australian Open seven times, US Open six times, French Open three times). Won sixteen Grand Slam doubles titles partnering her sister Venus. Also won three Olympic gold medals.

SERENA WILLIAMS WAS on the comeback trail. She was the most famous tennis player on the planet, but at the beginning of 2007 people had started to think that she was past her best.

She had taken six months off the previous year because

of injuries. She later revealed she had also been suffering from depression. Now she was back at the Australian Open, one of the biggest tournaments of the year.

In tennis, the four most important tournaments are called the Grand Slams and this was the first. Journalists were writing Serena off. They said she had no chance of getting to the top again. An article in a newspaper said:

"Williams is a lost cause."

Pat Cash, a famous Australian tennis player who had won the Wimbledon championship, said Serena was "deluded" for thinking she could become the world number one again. He said: "For all her talk Serena will never return to the top." Many agreed. She was only the world number 81 after all.

But now she was in the final in Australia against her arch-rival Maria Sharapova. The Russian was expected to win the Australian Open. She was the number one player and had been a star since she won Wimbledon three years earlier aged just seventeen, beating Serena in the final.

But Serena was determined. She had dealt with all sorts of criticism before and endured many injustices, including sexism and racism. People would also talk about how she looked in hurtful, ignorant and offensive ways. One writer even said she had "smothered" her looks in "an unsightly layer of thick muscled blubber".

What all these people had forgotten was that Serena had already proved herself to be one of the greatest sports stars of all time. With her older sister, Venus, she had ruled tennis. She had already won seven Grand Slam titles. Venus had won five. Tennis had never seen a sister act like this!

AND NOW SHE WAS BACK.

Everybody expected this to be a close final.

The old star (Serena) VS The new sensation (Sharapova)

Serena's critics were wrong. She started like the world number one instead of number 81. She hit the ball harder with her forehand than her backhand. Sharapova could not cope with Serena's booming serve. When Serena won 12 points in a row, she went 4–0 up. The 15,000 people watching in the stadium could not believe how easy it looked.

She was unstoppable.

Serena sometimes took notes onto the court to boost her confidence. This time the note had just one word on a piece of paper.

YETUNDE.

It was the name of her half-sister who had been murdered in 2003. After every two games the players changed ends and sat down to get their breath back and have a drink. Serena would get out her note and look at her half-sister's name. It motivated her even more.

She took the first set 6–1 and broke Sharapova's serve twice in the second. The final score was 6–1 6–2 and Serena collapsed to the floor and held her head in joy. The match had taken just 63 minutes.

When she was awarded the trophy on the court, she

fought back the tears. "I would like to dedicate this win to my sister, who's not here. Her name is Yetunde. I just love her so much. I said if I win this it's going to be for her. So thanks, Tunde."

Serena kept winning after Australia. She became the world number one again and won another fifteen Grand Slam titles.

★ ★ ★

EACH YEAR AT Wimbledon, the biggest tennis championship in the world, the stars would sit in a little theatre next to Centre Court after their matches for press conferences. Some were grumpy if they had lost. Some were funny. But when Serena entered the room there was an aura around her. She was an undisputed superstar.

I was lucky to go to many press conferences at Wimbledon over the years and listen to Serena tell her story.

The sisters grew up in Compton in Los Angeles, USA. The city is often associated with violent crime. But it was here that Serena's father, Richard, taught his daughters to play tennis. Venus and Serena had to scrape broken bottles and rubbish off the tennis court. And as they played, they ignored the police sirens.

But Richard was on a mission. He had watched tennis on TV and realized it could provide a better life for his daughters. His ambition became even stronger after Yetunde died.

Serena explained in interviews that she had not always been so confident. Just because you are successful does not mean you have no fears or problems.

When she was younger, Serena said she struggled with how she looked. People said nasty things about her because tennis had given her muscles. In an interview with ESPN, she said: "There was a time when I didn't feel incredibly comfortable about my body because I felt like I was too strong." But then she asked herself: "Who says I am too strong? This body has enabled me to be the greatest player I can be."

In another interview Serena admitted she had wanted to be like her sister. She spoke to a journalist from *Harper's Bazaar* and said:

"People would say I was born a guy, all because of my arms, or because I'm strong. I was different to Venus: she was thin and tall and beautiful, and I am strong and muscular."

She said she now knew who she was. She said she worked on her confidence every day. It was another form of training, just like hitting balls.

"You have to believe in yourself."

It took Serena time, but she became comfortable with herself. She said she did not look like every other girl and it took her a while to realize:

"Different is good."

If you lack confidence remember that even Serena Williams has to work at it. Serena posted an Instagram message explaining this to her twelve million followers. "I never let anything or anyone define me or my potential. I controlled my future."

You don't have to look like everyone else or do what everyone else does. You can control your future too. You just have to shut out the noise and trust yourself.

★ LEGEND LESSON ★

TAKE CONTROL.
Don't let others try to define you.
You are in charge of your own future.

205

LEGEND ID
MAGGIE ALPHONSI

BORN: 20 December 1983

NATIONALITY: British

SPORT: Rugby

LEGEND STATUS: Won the Rugby World Cup in 2014. Played 74 times for England. Member of the World Rugby Hall of Fame.

MAGGIE ALPHONSI WAS devastated when England lost the 2010 World Cup Final to New Zealand by just three points. That was four years ago. Now it was the 2014 final and Maggie was back. This time England were playing Canada in Paris. Maggie knew that England had to take their chances because Canada were a good team. There were close to 20,000 people in the stadium, but Maggie wasn't aware of them. She had the ball in her hands and she was running towards the line. This was it.

England and Canada had drawn 13–13 in the group stage just a week before. That had been bruising match. This time England's Emily Scarratt had already kicked two penalties to make it 6–0, as Maggie charged towards the line. There were just seven minutes to half-time. She had to get this right.

Maggie concentrated. As the defender came towards her she knew her timing needed to be perfect. She waited and told herself not to be impatient. And then, at just the right moment, she passed to her right. The defender realized that Maggie was going to pass too late. Danielle Waterman charged alongside Maggie and caught the pass. The defender could not get there. Danielle sprinted to the line and touched down.

11–0

But Canada refused to give up. Magali Harvey kicked three penalties and with 22 minutes left England's lead was only 11–9.

Maggie tried to stay calm. Ever since England had lost the last World Cup final, she had worked so hard to win this one. Her position was called flanker. She was one of the toughest players in the team. She was skilful and powerful. She knew she had to take charge.

Slowly England got on top. Emily kicked another penalty, but the killer blow came with just six minutes left. Emily spotted a gap and burst through the Canada defence to the line. Now they were there. A few minutes later the referee blew her whistle. The final score was 21–9.

MAGGIE WAS A WORLD CUP CHAMPION!

MAGGIE HAD OVERCOME a lot to reach the very top. She retired the following year and I interviewed her at the huge Twickenham stadium in London about her career and also her new life as a commentator for ITV Rugby. I wanted to know how a girl who had nearly been expelled from school had got to where she had.

We sat down in the hotel attached to the stadium and she told me she had been born with what doctors call a club foot. "My right foot was turned in," she said. "I had an operation when I was about one and then I was in and out of hospital." She walked differently and she said she had torn her hamstring muscle in the back of her leg five times as a result. That is not good news for a rugby player, but Maggie had spent twenty years not letting the problem stop her.

She was raised by her mum on an estate in north London. At school, she was always fighting and getting thrown out of lessons. Then she found rugby. She got the bus to training and said:

"The first time I made a tackle I loved it."

Her confidence grew because she had found something she was good at. It helped her at school too and she got her GCSEs. She told me:

"Rugby changed my life."

She explained that her girls' team would get a raw deal. They would have to play on the dodgy part of the pitch with dog poo, while the boys had the perfect surface. But she just worked on her own game. Slowly people began to realize that women were great rugby players too.

Now she was facing a new challenge by becoming the first ever former female player to commentate on men's international rugby. Some people had sent her horrible messages on social media. They said rugby was a man's game. One told her: "You belong in the kitchen". She was really nervous for her first match. Her confidence was low. So what did she do?

"I got the first question and I stopped thinking about gender and started thinking about the game. It kicked in that I'm very good at this sport. I've been doing it for 20 years. I won a World Cup which is more than most people can say."

It was interesting that Maggie was nervous after all she had achieved, but she was in a new environment. That can make anyone feel a bit uneasy. She reminded herself of her successes to boost her confidence. This is a key part of thinking more positively. Sometimes the mind is like a sieve and it only catches the negative thoughts. But if we remember past triumphs then it makes us feel better about ourselves and our ability to do something.

One of Maggie's tricks was to use positive phrases. These are called

MANTRAS.

Before going live on TV she would walk around and say phrases like this to herself:

"I am knowledgeable. I know my stuff."

She said she could even feel her body shape change when she felt completely confident. We can all learn from Maggie. Even a World Cup winner needs to feed her confidence with mantras, so there's no reason why we can't try this too.

Maggie was a huge success on TV. She ignored the criticism and realized the male presenters got it too.

"Someone has to be first, but once you take that step and take a battering other women will follow. Hopefully, one day I'll have 'The Maggie Alphonsi Show'."

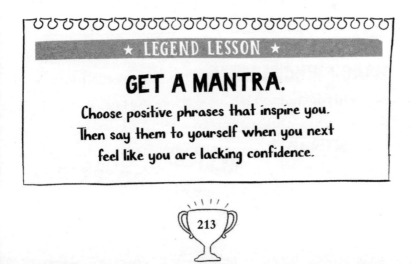

★ LEGEND LESSON ★

GET A MANTRA.

Choose positive phrases that inspire you. Then say them to yourself when you next feel like you are lacking confidence.

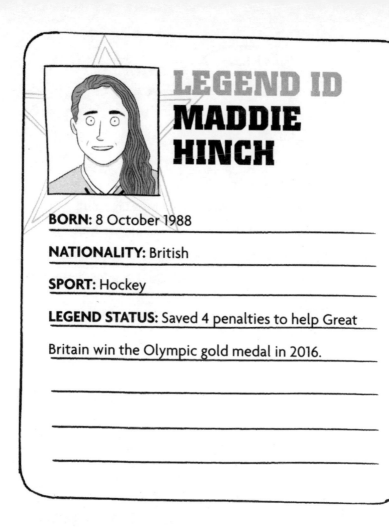

LEGEND ID
MADDIE HINCH

BORN: 8 October 1988

NATIONALITY: British

SPORT: Hockey

LEGEND STATUS: Saved 4 penalties to help Great Britain win the Olympic gold medal in 2016.

MADDIE HINCH LOOKED at her water bottle and read the words she had written on it before the final.

CHIN OUT! RELAX! HANDS UP!

It was up to her now. She was the goalkeeper for the Great Britain hockey team. The 2016 Olympic final in Rio de Janeiro, Brazil had finished 3–3 and now it was going to a penalty shoot-out. The Netherlands team were the favourites. Thousands of their fans dressed in orange were roaring in the grandstands. Maddie had to stay calm.

She went to the goal line and picked up her little black book. Inside were her notes about all the different players and where they liked to hit their penalties. She made sure the Netherlands players saw what she was doing because she wanted to plant a seed of doubt in their minds.

Each team had five penalties. Each player had to run from the 23-metre line with eight seconds to score. After all the work, the training and the matches, the team with most penalties in the next few minutes would become the Olympic champions.

Great Britain went first and missed. Now Maddie watched the first Netherlands player run straight towards her. Sometimes players tried to fool the goalkeeper or shift the ball to one side to create a better angle. This time the Netherlands player shot early.

Maddie flung out her legs and blocked the ball.

Alex Danson went next for GB and missed, but Maddie saved the second Netherlands one too. In fact, she saved it twice as the ball bounced back off her and the Netherlands player tried to hit the rebound high into the net. After two penalties each the shoot-out was 0–0. Then Sophie Bray scored to put Britain ahead.

But now a Netherlands player stepped forward who she did not recognize. Maddie had no notes about her in her black book. She told herself not to let that show and instead gave off an air of confidence. When the player darted to her right Maddie narrowed the angle and waited for the shot. It was hard and fast like a bullet. It struck her helmet and went wide. This was incredible.

She had saved three out of three penalties.

But when GB missed their fourth penalty they were still only 1–0 up.

CHIN OUT!

That was Maddie's reminder to herself to make herself look as big as possible. "Hands up" was the reminder to keep alert for the shot. "Relax" was the word she had written to keep loose and ready. You could feel the tension.

The fourth penalty did get past her but she had forced the striker wide and the shot hit the post and did not go in. It bounced back and Maddie kicked it clear. When Hollie Webb scored Britain's second penalty that was it.

They were the champions and

Maddie "Mad Dog" Hinch was the hero.

★ ★ ★

I WENT TO interview Maddie not long afterwards. She had moved to the Netherlands after the Olympics to play for one of the top hockey league sides there. I wanted to know how she had managed to become hockey's penalty queen.

She made a cup of coffee for me and the photographer, who had travelled with me, and we sat down at her kitchen table. First of all she explained the messages she wrote on her water bottle.

"They are codes. With 'chin out' I was reminding myself to put my chin forward because then your weight follows. When you are nervous or not confident you get tentative — the chin goes back and you become smaller."

Goalkeepers want to look big so that the penalty taker is the one feeling less confident.

Maddie also talked about the black notebook that she took onto the pitch with her. She said part of that was to make the penalty takers know that she had been studying them. She wanted to make them nervous.

When the player she did not know had stepped up she thought quickly. "You have to think on your feet. I thought,

Don't give it away that you don't know what to do? That was the closest one."

Maddie was trying to get inside the heads of her opponents. She was trying to unleash those inner chimps we've talked about. She wanted them to doubt themselves.

We can definitely use the trick she used with the player she had never seen before in our everyday lives.

The first step to confidence is sometimes pretending you have it!

Maddie said that penalties in all sport were about confidence. It is the same in football. It should be quite easy to score from twelve yards in football, but players often get nervous and start to think about what might go wrong. Some of the greatest footballers have missed important penalties. I asked her why this happened. "They are not suddenly bad footballers," she explained. "They just can't deliver in that moment."

Maddie said that the trick is to practise so often it becomes routine.

If you do that, you get something called muscle memory where your body is used to taking penalties and seeing them go in.

She said:

"You can't replicate the pressure of an Olympic shoot-out but you can get rid of it by being confident in your processes."

Then she said something fascinating:

"It's a mental thing not a skill thing. It's like an exam — if you've not done the homework then you get nervous and can't think straight."

For Maddie that was how she boosted her confidence. Her homework was the black book full of information on the opposing players. She studied it and felt great when she was under the most pressure. That is a valuable lesson. All the skill and talent in the world will not do you any good unless you have prepared your mind too.

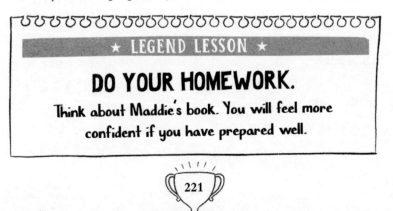

★ LEGEND LESSON ★

DO YOUR HOMEWORK.
Think about Maddie's book. You will feel more confident if you have prepared well.

LEGEND HEADLINES:

SPEED SKATING

Elise Christie is a brilliant Scottish speed skater but on the biggest stages, things never quite went to plan. She was the reigning 1,000 metres world champion when she went to the 2014 Winter Olympics in Sochi, Russia. She was disqualified in all three of her races after two collisions with other skaters. Four years later in PyeongChang, South Korea at the 2018 Winter Olympics, she fell three times. She was a three-time world champion, but it just had not come right when she wanted. "Self-confidence is what really counts," she said. "Acceptance of what you've been through is key."

FOOTBALL

There are lots of ways to take penalties. Some players pick a spot. Others wait until the last moment for the goalkeeper to dive. Some just go for power. In the 2012 European Championships quarter-final against England, Italian **Andrea Pirlo** did something amazing. Under intense pressure, the Italian calmly chipped the ball down the middle of the goal to score. He explained the England goalkeeper Joe Hart was throwing his arms around trying to distract him. He thought Hart was so worked up he would put all his energy into a big dive. Pirlo's confidence came from keeping cool under pressure.

THE CONFIDENCE TRICK

ATHLETICS

Jessica Ennis-Hill was at her lowest ebb in 2008. She had been preparing for the heptathlon at the Olympic Games in Beijing, China, when she felt a pain in her ankle. She got it checked out and was told that she had a broken foot and would miss the heptathlon. She was crushed because she had been working for years to get to Beijing. Now her dream was over. Eventually, she reset her goals and rebuilt her confidence. Four years later she was fit and she won the gold medal for Great Britain at the 2012 Olympics in London.

FOOTBALL

Mia Hamm was one of the first superstar women's footballers. She played for the USA for seventeen years and scored 158 goals. In 2004, FIFA produced a list of the 125 greatest players in the world. Mia was one of only two women on the list. Thanks to her women's football is now much more popular and respected. She says football is where she found her self-belief. "I was a really shy kid from a military family so we moved every two or three years," she said. "Sport was an easy way to make a connection. It really helped give me confidence."

CHAPTER 6:
NEVER GIVE UP

If you think everything is against you, remember Louis Zamperini.

We have already covered the 1936 Olympics when Jesse Owens won four gold medals in front of Adolf Hitler. Louis Zamperini was one of Jesse's American teammates. He stayed in the same cottage and swiped the "DO NOT DISTURB" sign off Jesse's door as a joke. Jesse was soon surrounded by autograph hunters as a result!

Louis made the final of the 5,000 metres. The best runners in that event were from Finland and it was clear from the bell to signal the start of the last lap that Louis was not going to get a medal. But instead of giving up he remembered what his brother Pete had said:

"A lifetime of glory is worth a moment of pain."

He ran as fast as he could and made up 50 metres on the last lap. He came eighth but it was his best-ever-time.

Louis thought his time would come at the next Olympics in 1940, but the Games were cancelled because of the Second World War. So Louis became a pilot in the American air force. In 1944, his plane crashed into the Pacific Ocean 528 miles off the shore of Japan, one of the USA's war-time enemies. He survived, but spent 47 days on a life raft without food or water. First, the raft was attacked by sharks. Then it was attacked by a Japanese fighter plane, which fired bullets at him. he had no choice but to jump in the sea to hide and hope the sharks would not get him by the time the plane had gone. Finally, he made it to the Japanese shore.

But his ordeal was not over. Louis was taken to a prisoner of war camp where the conditions were brutal. He spent two years there, but he never gave up hope. The war ended in 1945. He was freed and made it back to the USA. He got married and was still skateboarding at the age of 85.

Sport – and life – is full of stories of people who never gave up.

We have already met some of them. Derek Redmond did not give up when he was injured during the biggest race of his life. Lionel Messi did not give up when he was diagnosed with a hormone deficiency. Tanni Grey-Thompson did not give up on sport because she had spina bifida.

Most of us will never be world champions or famous sports stars, but when the going gets tough, adopting the mindeset of a legend will change your perspective.

There is a saying in athletics:

LEAVE IT ALL ON THE TRACK.

This means give it absolutely everything. Never do something half-heartedly. If you put all your effort into a task then you will have no regrets. You don't want to finish a race and then think you could have gone faster. You want to do what Louis Zamperini did. He was only eighth in that final in 1936, but he had done his very best and was proud.

Sometimes your best will not be good enough to win. Even Lionel Messi knows that. He said:

"You have to accept you can't win all the time."

But there are tricks that the sports stars can teach us about not giving up.

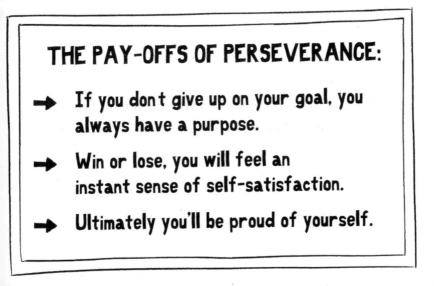

THE PAY-OFFS OF PERSEVERANCE:

➡ **If you don't give up on your goal, you always have a purpose.**

➡ **Win or lose, you will feel an instant sense of self-satisfaction.**

➡ **Ultimately you'll be proud of yourself.**

Let's look at the marathon. It takes an average of 40,000 steps to complete a marathon, which is 26.2 miles.

If you think about just how far you have to run to complete a marathon, it is easy to put away your trainers and stop running altogether. Believe me, I've been there.

But if you break the distance down into mini goals it gets a whole lot easier.

Instead of thinking about 26.2 miles, many runners split the distance down into four bits of 6.5 miles.

A -- B

26 long, hard miles

A ---------- B ---------- C ---------- D ---------- E for END

1st bit   2nd bit   3rd bit   Last bit

Any massive goal is easier if you break it down into doable chunks. Rather than giving up, think about how you can turn your challenge into a series of stepping stones. That way you will end your challenge with a feeling of pride and satisfaction in giving it everything you could.

In this chapter we will see what happened when our sports legends did not give up, however long and hard the road in front of them looked.

We will meet the refugee who lost his home, his family and even his country before making it as a footballer. He said the secret to not giving up is to

There is the kickboxer who was so ill she could not get out of bed for months before recovering to win a world title. She managed to

FIND A HAPPY PLACE.

We will join the football team who were down and out in the biggest match of their lives but came back to win. They showed

IT'S NEVER TOO LATE.

Now that's good news!

And finally we will learn about the world's greatest gymnast who had to endure a troubled childhood and an abusive coach, but still achieved amazing things. She was able to

BE THE INSPIRATION.

LEGEND ID
BAYAN MAHMUD

BORN: 15 December 1994

NATIONALITY: Ghanaian

SPORT: Football

LEGEND STATUS: Signed for Boca Juniors in Argentina. Then played professional football in France.

BAYAN MAHMUD WAS ten years old when he sensed something was wrong. He rushed to his house in the town of Bawku in Ghana where his older brother Muntala was crying. There had been an attack. Muntala hugged Bayan and slowly explained what had happened.

In their region, there were two groups of people, the Kusai and the Mamprusi, who had been fighting each other for years. Each wanted to be in charge. Bayan's family belonged to the Kusai, but while he had been away the Mamprusi had killed lots of people including Bayan's parents. Bayan looked at Muntala. Their world had suddenly collapsed.

This tragedy was the start of an unbelievable journey.

For five years, the brothers lived in an orphanage. But the fighting between the Kusai and the Mamprusi continued in Ghana. Bayan tried not to think about his parents because it made him too sad. He hoped that things might get better and people would live in peace.

One day he heard that the Mamprusi were coming back. Bayan was terrified. He fled to the road out of town, but lost his brother in the confusion. A truck was passing and stopped. The man said he was going to the Cape Coast. Anywhere was fine for Bayan. He thought about Muntala, but he had to escape.

When the man dropped him off, he was alone and scared. He lived rough by the docks. Some other street

231

children helped him and gave him a few crumbs of food. They made a small amount of money by tying up boats. Bayan said he dreamt of getting to Europe and starting a new life there. The boys said they could smuggle him onto a boat.

Bayan was only fifteen. He had no idea where he was going, but one night he hid among the giant steel containers on the ship as it left the dock. The boat was a scary place.

He feared that if he was found he would be thrown overboard.

One night a crew member did find him. Bayan was terrified, but the man took pity on him. He kept him hidden and gave him some food. "Do you even know where you are going?" the man asked Bayan. He shook his head.

The enormous ship sailed on. It was cold and the waves sounded like thunder as they crashed against the steel hull. Finally, after what seemed like for ever, the boat stopped. Bayan did not know where he was and did not understand the language. It was only later that he realized he was not in Europe at all.

He had spent months at sea only to end up in Argentina. The ship had travelled all the way from Africa up the Paraná River to the port of Rosario, the same city where Lionel Messi had grown up.

Bayan lived on the streets again. Another stranger helped him. He said Bayan should go to Buenos Aires, the capital of Argentina. The stranger said there were lots of African people there and they would help him. The stranger then paid for his bus ticket.

When he got to Buenos Aires, Bayan was on the streets once more. A couple of boys took him to the immigration centre, for people who had come to the country. From there, Bayan was sent to a refugee camp with others who had fled their countries because of war and disasters.

Life in the camp was a struggle. The only fun Bayan had was when a group of men asked him to play football with them in one of the city squares. Bayan was fast and skilful and the men paid him 20 pesos (about 20 pence) to play.

One day, a man was watching. It changed Bayan's life.

He was called Ruben and he told Bayan that he was
a very talented player. He said he should go for a trial at a
local club. Ruben said he knew the right people. Before
long, Bayan was at Boca Juniors. Even Bayan had heard of
Boca. They were one of the most famous clubs in all of
South America!

Bayan was nervous on the day of his trial but he thought about how far he had come. He had got through things that were much worse. So he went out onto the pitch and played brilliantly. He was picked and offered a contract. He moved from the refugee camp to the club's training camp. Finally, he had a home. People even began to ask for his autograph. The night after he was picked Bayan went home and cried. This time they were tears of joy.

★ ★ ★

IT WAS A dramatic story. When I heard it I decided I wanted to meet Bayan. I wanted to know how he had kept going. After lots of phone calls, I finally sat down with him on a bench by a tree in a peaceful square near Boca Juniors' ground. He had a red T-shirt, white shorts and a big smile.

He told me about the tragedy when his home was attacked. "The Mamprusi have a mark on their body. I don't have it, so they knew I was not one of them. I feared for my life." He was terrified.

"My mind was on fire so I fled."

He still remembered the kindness of the man on the boat. "He saved me," he said. "I owe him everything."

But when he got to Argentina he was still unhappy. "I went back to living on the street again. That was hard. I thought about my brother a lot and I cried a lot."

He had never given up hope. Whenever things were bad he told himself to think positively. Instead of telling himself how terrible things were, he thought of all the people who had helped him – the street kids, the man on the boat, the stranger who put him on the bus, the man in the square.

I said goodbye to Bayan who had to get ready for training. He was grateful for his opportunity and I was grateful for the chance to meet him.

However bad things can get it is important to cling to hope and be grateful for the good things. Remember Pete Reed who had won three Olympic gold medals and suddenly could not walk? Instead of feeling bad, he was just grateful that he could still use his arms. That attitude helped his rehabilitation. You can be grateful for little things like a sunny day or big things like friends and family.

This is something champions do too. They do not dwell on setbacks. They imagine good things happening. Remember Chris Hoy, the cyclist, imagining the perfect race? The more you think about a good outcome the more it seems normal.

Just before we met, Bayan said he had found out from social media that his brother was still alive. He said: "Football has given me a dream that is priceless."

I left Bayan feeling inspired. In fact, I still have his picture on my office wall at home!

★ LEGEND LESSON ★

BE GRATEFUL.

There are always things to be thankful for so look for the positive and stay hopeful.

LEGEND ID
RUQSANA BEGUM

BORN: 15 October 1983

NATIONALITY: British

SPORT: Kick-boxing/boxing

LEGEND STATUS: Won the Muay Thai World Kick-boxing title in 2016.

THIS WAS HER last chance. It was 2015 and Ruqsana Begum was fighting for the Muay Thai World Kick-boxing title for the third time. She had been winning the first fight when her opponent landed a foot on her. That had made her dizzy and her coach stopped the fight. The second time she thought she had won, but the judges awarded the fight to her opponent. Now she looked across the ring at her bigger Swedish rival, Susanna Salmijärvi.

IT WAS NOW OR NEVER.

Rox, as everyone called her, had a huge challenge to overcome. She suffered from an illness called ME. This is also known as chronic fatigue syndrome and it left her feeling exhausted. The fight had already been postponed once because of her illness. Now she wondered if she could last five two-minute rounds. The crowd in the Hackney arena in London were roaring. She knew she had to try and stop her rival early. She said to herself: "Go for it!"

Rox attacked from the start. She threw punches with both hands. She kicked too. When Susanna tried to kick back, Rox caught her leg and dumped her on the canvas.

It was a hard fight, but few people watching knew just what Rox had gone through to be here.

Once she had been so ill, she had to spend weeks in bed.

And then just a few hours before this fight she had been suffering with a fever. "Get to the venue and see how you feel," her coach said.

She tried to imagine herself better.

Now she could feel her power coming back. She was landing good shots and scoring points. Finally, the end came. Rox raised her hands, but so did the Swede. It would go to the judges to decide who was the winner.

Rox held her breath. The referee stood between the two women. When the announcer read out Rox's name she shut her eyes in relief. Finally she was the world champion.

★ ★ ★

I WANTED TO interview Rox as soon as I heard her story. How could someone who was so ill they couldn't leave their bed become a kick-boxing world champion? I went to London and found the address of her gym. It was like a rabbit hole, tucked underneath some railway arches.

As we talked she broke down and cried on several occasions.

She had an amazing story that included elements from every chapter in this book.

Rox has Bangladeshi heritage and her parents felt it was important for their daughters to cook and help their mother at home. But when Rox was seventeen, she saw an advert for a kick-boxing class and was intrigued. She went to the gym and liked it. It was noisy, dingy and smelt of stale sweat, but she felt comfortable there.

She worried that her parents would stop her kick-boxing because it was not what Muslim girls traditionally did. She didn't tell them she had taken up the sport and wore long sleeves to cover her bruises.

In keeping with her cultural tradition, her parents chose

241

a man to be her husband. Once she was married, she moved in with her husband and his parents, but hated it. "I felt like a slave," she told me. "I felt bullied. I felt really down. One day I was peeling prawns in the kitchen. I thought, *This is my life.* That was when I collapsed."

She was diagnosed with ME, which left her physically and mentally exhausted. After a few days in hospital, she went back to her parents' house. She spent four months in bed due to ME and her husband did not visit her once. They got divorced. Rox's confidence was shattered.

"I lost my job, my marriage and myself. From being a confident young woman, I didn't even know what colour I liked. I didn't know who I was. The only thing I knew was this place."

"This place" was the gym. Finally, Rox plucked up the courage to tell her parents the truth. She even took them to the gym to meet her coach, Bill. Rox was taking antidepressant tablets to help her mental health, and her parents were very worried about her. They just wanted her to be well again and could see the gym was the only thing that seemed to build her confidence.

Even with her parents' approval, it wasn't easy. Some of the other women in the gym did not include her. Once they all went to a birthday party, but did not invite Rox.

"I don't think some of them ever accepted me. I wondered if it was because I was the only Asian girl. Was it because I was a Muslim?"

She kept going, even though her ME sometimes meant she was so drained of energy she could not lift her arms. Eventually, the women who excluded her all left the gym.

ROX BECAME THE STAR.

"It just shows that where the mind goes the body will follow," she said. "At first my doctor told me I could do no sport at all." But Rox discovered:

"It was me against myself."

This is a battle we all face at times. It is

You vs your inner chimp.

You vs the negative voice inside your head.

Rox didn't quit the battle. She never gave up and overcame her challenges by getting help and finding a happy place. For her, it was the gym where she could forget all the bad things and focus on her sport. For us it might be a friend or a hobby or even a favourite TV show. If you have something that helps you forget your problems for a bit, it can recharge your batteries and help you face them again when you are ready.

And finally, in that ring in Hackney, fighting for the world title, Rox was ready.

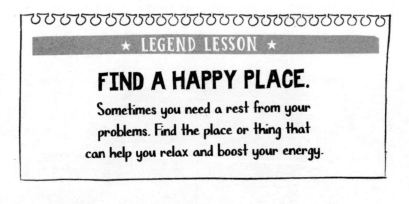

★ LEGEND LESSON ★

FIND A HAPPY PLACE.

Sometimes you need a rest from your problems. Find the place or thing that can help you relax and boost your energy.

LEGEND ID
LIVERPOOL

FOUNDED: 1892

NATIONALITY: British

SPORT: Football

LEGEND STATUS: Won more games in the top division than any other. Champions of England nineteen times. Won the European Cup/Champions League six times. Won the FA Cup six times.

AT HALF-TIME in the Champions League Final in 2005 Liverpool's players sat in the dressing room with their heads down. They were being thrashed. It was 3–0 to AC Milan.

It had taken the Italian giants less than one minute to score the first goal!

Up in the broadcasting booth, the man commentating for BBC Radio said: "This game is over." And then through the door came a familiar sound. It grew louder and louder and the players looked at each other.

Around 30,000 Liverpool fans had travelled to Istanbul, Turkey for the final and they put their disappointment to one side to get behind their team and sing their famous club anthem. Listening up in the press box, it sent shivers down the spine.

"YOU'LL NEVER WALK ALONE!"

Rafa Benítez was the Liverpool manager. He knew he had to pick his words carefully. He needed to inspire his team. Some players probably thought it was impossible to come back from 3–0 against a team as good as AC Milan.

"We have nothing to lose. If we can relax we can get a goal. And if we get the first goal we can come back into the game. We have to fight. We owe something to the supporters. Don't let your heads drop. You have to hold your heads high for the supporters. Fight for 45 minutes. If we score, we are in it."

Then Rafa said:

"If you believe we can do it, we can do it. Give yourselves the chance to be heroes."

The players looked at him. It was hard to think they could score four goals, but maybe they could get one. And get the first goal and you never know.

It was interesting that Rafa told his players that they had nothing to lose. It made them think that if they did anything good in the second half that was a bonus. Suddenly the players relaxed. They were not scared of making a mistake.

Steven Gerrard was the captain and a local Liverpool boy. After 54 minutes he ran into the area. His looping header arced into the net.

3—1

Now they had their goal and a chance. Two minutes later Vladimír Šmicer struck a low shot from a long way out. Dida, the Milan goalkeeper, dived but could not get there in time.

3—2

Now *everybody* believed. The fans were going crazy. A team that had looked defeated by half-time were now attacking Milan. The Milan players looked shocked.

Gerrard saw a chance. He ran into the box and saw the goal looming. Then he felt a shove in his back and he went flying to the ground. The entire crowd held its breath before the referee pointed to the spot.

PENALTY!!!

Imagine the pressure on Xabi Alonso, Liverpool's Spanish midfielder. He tried to shut out the noise, but it was hard. This was their golden chance. He put the ball on the penalty spot and trotted up. He struck the ball cleanly with his right foot but to his horror he saw Dida, the Milan keeper, diving the right way. The keeper stopped the shot. But Xabi was not finished. He followed up and swung his left boot at the rebound. The ball shot into the roof of the net.

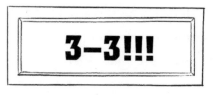

3–3!!!

It had taken only six minutes to wipe away Milan's lead.

SIX MINUTES TO DO THE IMPOSSIBLE.

They were level but the game still had to be won. There were no more goals and so the match went to extra time – two halves of fifteen minutes.

With just three minutes of extra time left, another miracle happened. Milan's striker, Andriy Shevchenko was one of the greatest in the world. The season before he had won the Ballon d'Or and he was the FIFA world player of the year. During his career he scored more than 300 goals. Now, with the clock ticking, he had his chance. A cross came in and he met it perfectly with his head. He aimed downwards like he had been taught.

Somehow the Liverpool goalkeeper, Jerzy Dudek, managed to stop it. But the rebound was coming straight back to Shevchenko.

He was only five yards from the goal. Dudek was still on the ground. The watching Liverpool players felt their hearts sink. All that work looked like being for nothing.

The radio commentator next to me shouted:

"THE GOAL IS AT HIS MERCY!"

Shevchenko shot. But somehow Dudek put his head and his hands in the way and managed to deflect the ball over the top. The commentator yelled:

251

"THAT IS
BEYOND BELIEF!"

Shevchenko certainly could not believe it. He held his head. He still could not believe it when asked about it afterwards.

The match ended 3–3. That meant a penalty shoot-out, but Liverpool felt fate was on their side now. They had momentum. Events were going their way.

Milan missed their first two penalties and Liverpool scored theirs. After four shots each, Liverpool were 3–2 up, which meant that when Shevchenko stepped up he had to score or Liverpool had won.

He was good at penalties, but the pressure was huge. When Dudek saved, Shevchenko blasted the rebound over the bar in anger. The Liverpool players ran to Dudek to celebrate.

★ ★ ★

IT WAS AMAZING. I saw Steven Gerrard down in the stadium later that night with the European Cup. The journalists asked him questions and jostled each other to get the best position as they held their tape recorders near to him. He still looked like he was in a daze.

252

Gerrard had known that when Liverpool were losing 3–0, it was only half-time. It's never too late and all you can do in anything is to try your best. The first step for Liverpool was to get one goal and stop being embarrassed. When they got a second goal they began to believe they could win.

We can learn from what happened that night. If something seems impossible don't give up. Find a small target to start with. Pretend you have nothing to lose. Remove the pressure. The night became known as

THE MIRACLE OF ISTANBUL.

Katarina Johnson-Thompson is a Liverpool fan. She said she used the game as inspiration when she was going through bad times in athletics. "It affected me deeply," she said. "It was like 'never count us out'. The club has been through a lot but always comes back." We should tell ourselves the same thing: never count us out.

★ LEGEND LESSON ★

IT'S NEVER TOO LATE.
You have to keep going because amazing things sometimes happen.

LEGEND ID
SIMONE BILES

BORN: 14 March 1997

NATIONALITY: American

SPORT: Gymnastics

LEGEND STATUS: Won four gold medals at the 2016 Olympic Games and has a record nineteen world titles. Considered the greatest gymnast of all time.

SIMONE BILES WAS already the star of the 2016 Olympic Games in Rio de Janeiro, Brazil. She was nineteen and only 4 feet 8 inches tall, but she was a giant. Everybody wanted to see her compete. Even though I wasn't covering the gymnastics in Brazil that year, I made sure I went to the

Arena Olímpica do Rio one night. It's not every day you got the chance to see a legend in action.

At home in the USA, everyone was going wild. Simone had already won three gold medals in different events and had appeared on the front of the prestigious *Time* magazine. A video of her winking and smiling in Rio, taken earlier in the week, had been viewed eleven million times on social media.

She even had her own emoji called the Simoji.

The floor exercise was the discipline that most people remembered. This was her favourite event and she was determined to get it right.

Her performance was amazing.

She was small but she could leap higher than everyone else. She had her own signature move too. It was called

THE BILES.

This was when she took off backwards and did a double backward somersault and a half-twist that meant she landed facing forwards. It was stunning to watch, and along with the crowd, I leapt to my feet to applaud her.

When the music finally stopped, Simone smiled. She knew she had done enough, but waited for the scores to flash up.

15.966

That was a huge score!

The next best was her USA teammate Aly Raisman who had won silver with 15.500.

Her performance meant that she was the first woman to win four gold medals at a single Olympic Games for 35 years.

"It's crazy to think what I've done," she said to the journalists.

★ ★ ★

IT WAS SENSATIONAL and Simone became one of the most famous sports stars in the world after that.

But Simone had only got here because she never gave up. She had not had an easy life. When she was little her mother had become addicted to drugs and alcohol. One day, when she was only three, a lady arrived at her home in Ohio. She told Simone and her three siblings that they were being taken into care because her mother couldn't look after them. They went to live with foster parents.

The social worker contacted Simone's grandfather, who lived far away in Texas. When he heard what had happened to Simone, he wanted to help. He and his wife took in the four children.

But Simone faced more challenges. She said: "Growing

up it was kind of a struggle being so small. Everyone would make fun of me."

Even then, she managed to turn it to her advantage and said her height allowed her to get into secret places when playing hide and seek.

She started gymnastics on a daycare field trip when she was six. She was a natural and joined a club. She had to make lots of sacrifices and started being homeschooled so she could spend more time practising.

There were injuries and setbacks. She felt self-conscious because some of the people at school would talk about her big muscles, just like others had done about Serena Williams. Far worse, a coach abused Simone and many of her USA gymnastics teammates. Eventually, when Simone and others very bravely spoke out in 2018, the coach was sent to jail.

Despite everything, Simone wanted to inspire more girls. When she was growing up, she was one of the few Black gymnasts. In one interview she said: "I feel like I have instilled confidence in little African Americans all over the world."

Our goals may not be as huge as the ones Simone had, but they are just as important to us. A test or a football match can be our Olympic Games. And, with the right people to inspire you, and act as your role models, you can succeed too. As Simone said:

"If I can do it then so can you."

Simone took a break from gymnastics but in 2019 she was back at the World Artistic Gymnastics Championships in Qatar. There she faced another challenge. She was in serious pain and rushed to hospital where she was diagnosed with kidney stones. Most people would have given up at that point. Not Simone. She decided she could not let her team down. She checked herself out of hospital and a day later helped the USA win the team gold medal!

She is one of the most inspiring figures in this book. She could have given up many times. But she kept going and managed to overcome all obstacles to win four Olympic and a staggering nineteen world titles. Her secret?

"If you ever have a mistake you try to just kind of forget about it because if you carry that with you for the rest of the routine then it might not go as planned. So you just kind of shake it off."

That is good advice when we feel like something is too hard. Lots of people give up after making one mistake. So if you decide to carry on you are already ahead of the game. And let's leave the last word to the truly, astoundingly brilliant Simone Biles, an inspiration to us all:

"I'd rather regret the risk that didn't work out than the chances I didn't take."

★ LEGEND LESSON ★

BE THE INSPIRATION.

You don't have to be brilliant but if you keep trying you will inspire others.

LEGEND HEADLINES:

CRICKET

England were almost down and out in the third Ashes Test match against arch-rivals Australia in 2019. They had needed to get a record score of 359 to catch Australia. Their last two batsmen were **Ben Stokes**, a fierce competitor, and Jack Leach, a bowler not expected to get many runs. When Jack came in England still needed 73. In their first innings the team had managed just 67 runs altogether. It looked hopeless and nobody gave them a chance, but Ben took control and started to hit sixes and fours. By the end, he was so exhausted he could barely lift his bat, but he scored 135 not out to give England their most famous win.

ATHLETICS

The indigenous people of Australia are called Aborigines and throughout history they have been persecuted for being different. Australian athlete **Cathy Freeman's** grandmother was taken from her parents and placed with a white family. People had refused to get in a car with Cathy or hand her trophies because of who she was. She could have given up, but Cathy won gold in the 400 metres at the 2000 Olympics in Sydney. She became a superstar and used her platform to highlight the way the Aboriginal people were discriminated against. She showed that everyone deserves respect and a chance.

NEVER GIVE UP

FOOTBALL

In the 1999 Champions League Final, Bayern Munich were beating **Manchester United** 1–0. The 90 minutes had finished and the referee added on a few minutes for stoppages. Manchester had been losing since the sixth minute. But after 90 minutes and 36 seconds, Teddy Sheringham scored. The game now looked like going to extra time. Then at 92 minutes and 17 seconds, David Beckham took the last corner. Teddy headed the ball and Ole Gunnar Solskjær prodded the ball in. The Bayern Munich ribbons had already been fixed to the cup so they had to be quickly replaced with Manchester's colours.

NETBALL

England had not beaten Australia for five years when they faced them in the Commonwealth Games final in 2018. The match took place in Australia so the crowd were cheering for the home side. Early in the fourth period England were four goals down but they managed to level the scores at 51–51 with 20 seconds left. Then, with one second left, Helen Housby had the chance to win the match. She made no mistake and brought the gold home for England. The England coach Tracey Neville is the sister of Gary and Phil Neville, part of the Manchester United team who beat Bayern Munich in the 1999 Champions League Final.

LEGENDS IN BRIEF
NEVER GIVE UP

Athletics

Richard Whitehead was already a star after winning the 200 metres in the T42 class at the 2012 Paralympics in London. It was not enough for the man who had been born without legs and ran on artificial limbs. His plan was to use his fame to raise money for charity. So the next year he set off on a 977 mile race along the length of Britain. His plan was to run 40 marathons in 40 days. I met him halfway and the stumps where his artificial legs were attached were blistered and sore, but he wasn't going to quit. He had a tattoo on his arm saying:

"COMETH THE HOUR COMETH THE MAN."

He reached his target and raised more than £100,000.

YOU CAN DO IT TOO!

THERE ARE LOTS of incredible stories that I did not have room for in this book.

I will never forget going to the Czech Republic to meet an old lady called Dana Zátopková. She was 92 and had won a gold medal at throwing the javelin at the 1952 Olympic Games in Helsinki, Finland. Her husband, a famous runner called Emil Zátopek, had won a gold medal on the same day. Imagine that.

Emil had died a long time ago, but Dana told me how he had become a superstar after he won three gold medals at one Olympics. But when he had retired, Russia invaded his country and he went down to the square in Prague, where he lived, and stood in front of the tanks. He refused to let them past. Emil ended up being punished and sent to work down a mine, but he always did what was right. He had been brave as a runner and he was brave in all other areas of his life.

In the corner of Dana's little flat was her old javelin from the Olympics. I looked at it and imagined being back in 1952. I will treasure that meeting forever.

On another day I met a famous motorcycle racer called Barry Sheene. He had been the world champion but was actually more famous for crashing at world record speed. He could have been killed but he survived falling at 175 mph.

He suffered broken bones in his thigh, arm and leg. He had to have a 46-centimetre steel rod put in his thigh, but he came back to win again. Barry did not like it when people treated him differently. When people called him a legend he laughed.

"I can't stand people who are legends in their own lunchtime," he said. "I'm the sort of bloke who, if you've got time for me, I've got time for you."

What he meant was that it's nice to be important, but it's more important to be nice. And that is something that I think we should always remember. Sport is not just about being mega-famous and winning things. It's all about how it makes you feel. Most importantly, it's about having fun. It doesn't matter if you are a footballer playing in the World Cup final or having a kickaround in the park. If you are giving it your all and enjoying yourself, that's all that matters.

I hope these stories have inspired you and that you might use the legends' advice to be the best that you can be.

Don't be afraid. All these people have made mistakes. All faced hurdles. Lots were criticized. Some were called names. All became great in their own way and they all did their best which is all that we can do.

Be inspired and take that first small step to reaching the top of your own world.

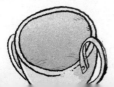

ACKNOWLEDGEMENTS

I would like to thank Debs, Erin and Sam for their support and to apologize to Dougie the dog for not including any greyhound racing in *Sports Legends*. Also, thanks to Daisy Jellicoe for being a brilliant editor, Chloé Tartinville for her amazing work on the design and James Davies for his fantastic illustrations. Finally, I hope this book inspires Leeds United to win the Champions League – one day.

RICK BROADBENT

Rick Broadbent has travelled all over the world to watch sport and write about it. He has written books about athletics, football, motorsport and a man who lived with an orangutan. The best thing he has seen in sport is Usain Bolt breaking the 100 metres world record in China at the 2008 Beijing Olympics, but it was a long way to go for ten seconds of action!